THE FIRST 60 YEARS

ALISTAIR DEAYTON & IAIN QUINN

IN ASSOCIATION WITH PATRICK MURRELL

AMBERLEY

ACKNOWLEDGEMENTS

Special thanks must be given to Patrick Murrell, for help with information and the use of photographs on the Bristol Channel area. The authors' sincere thanks for the use of photographs also go to George Boswell, Ian Somerville, Bill Backshell, Bryan Kennedy, Frank Gradwell, Chris Jones, John Newth, John Crae, Charles McCrossan, Matt Verrall, Mike Tedstone, Tony Horn, Campbell McCutcheon, the late Hamish Stewart and John Ramsey and William M. Worden for the use of a photograph from the late Gordon P. Bugbee's collection. Many illustrations have also come from the authors' own extensive collections.

The authors extend their thanks to the captains, crews and company directors of both Waverley Steam Navigation and Waverley Excursions Ltd, for giving the enthusiasts and public at large many rare and wonderful voyages on board this classic coastal steamer. We acknowledge Ian Ramsay (WSN) for his very fine foreword.

If you would like to add a place, pier or harbour to the gazetteer in case we have missed any, please inform us, and any additions will be incorporated in future editions of this book

Cover Illustration: *Balmoral* and *Waverley*, Britain's last surviving coastal pleasure steamers, off Penarth on 26 May 2004.

First published 2009

Amberley Publishing
Cirencester Road, Chalford,
Stroud, Gloucestershire, GL6 8PE

www.amberley-books.com

Copyright © Alistair Deayton & Iain Quinn 2009

The right of Alistair Deayton & Iain Quinn to be identified as the Author of this work has been asserted in accordance with the Copyrights, Designs and Patents Act 1988.

British Library Cataloguing in Publication Data.
A catalogue record for this book is available from the British Library.

ISBN 978 1 84868 426 3

Typesetting and Origination by Amberley Publishing.
Printed in Great Britain.

CONTENTS

FOREWORD
Balmoral's Diamond Jubliee Year

Alistair Deayton and Iain Quinn are to be congratulated for compiling such a splendid record of *Balmoral's* sixty glorious and much-travelled years. To those of us who sail on her, and know her unique charms, it is pleasing, but not surprising, to know that in her coastwise travels she has been able to give so much pleasure to so many people, and to enlist them into her fan club.

Looking at this excellent selection of photographs in this, her diamond jubilee year, one is struck by the many and diverse ports with which she has become familiar during the various stages of her operating life. Firstly, she was an all-year work-horse for her original owners, the Red Funnel fleet, operating out of Southampton to the Isle of Wight, and had a secondary role as an excursion steamer in summer. Some twenty years at Southampton were followed by a lengthy spell as an excursion vessel on the Bristol Channel, under the famous Campbell house flag, until the sad decline of the excursion business.

The next stage as a floating restaurant at Dundee is best forgotten, but at least the ship was still in a sufficiently good condition for the Waverley organisation to purchase her in 1985 and steam her, via the Pentland Firth, to Glasgow for refurbishment. Since her return to passenger service under the Waverley house flag, she has become a 'weel kent' vessel at ports all around the Great Britain, Ireland and the Isle of Man – with a couple of continental trips thrown in for good measure. In the course of her travels she has circumnavigated Britain several times. On one occasion, when the writer was onboard for the passage between Llandudno and Granton, we ran out of water about Cape Wrath! Ever tried washing and shaving on Diet Coke or Lilt? Neither have I!

Balmoral is now the mainstay of cruising on the Bristol Channel, but she also operates regularly on the South Coast, the Thames and Irish Sea, with occasional forays to the East Coast and the Clyde. At all these places she has gained a special place in the hearts of excursionists and supporters alike.

So I hope that you will enjoy looking at these superb photographs, and that it will make you determined to experience the pleasure of sailing on board *Balmoral* in all its glorious reality – and from 'a port near you'. Because, if *Balmoral* is to be around for a few more decades, she will need us to support her, by ensuring that we make the effort to cross her gangplank as frequently as we can.

Ian Ramsay
Director
Waverley Steam Navigation Company Ltd

MV *Balmoral*
A Brief History

The Red Funnel Years

Balmoral was ordered in 1947, the year *Waverley* entered service. On a boiling hot day in June 1949 she was launched from the Woolston yard of J.I. Thornycroft. By December she was in service on Red Funnel's car and passenger service from Southampton (Royal Pier) to Cowes, Isle of Wight. Red Funnel has the longest company name ever registered in the UK: the Southampton, Isle of Wight and South of England Royal Mail Steam Packet Company. The company has been known as Red Funnel since the red and black funnel colours were adopted in 1935.

Trials were run in late October and early November 1949. *Balmoral* measured 736 gross tons, and had two six-cylinder Newbury Sirron diesel engines. In 2003 she was re-engined with Danish-built Grenaa diesels whilst under WSN ownership.

As well as operating the ferry service to the Isle of Wight, she was a delightful pleasure vessel and ran trips to Ryde, Sandown, Shanklin, Ventnor and round the Isle of Wight, also serving Southsea. She also provided an opportunity to view the many classic liners arriving and departing from the port of Southampton, including the Cunard giants *Queen Mary* and *Queen Elizabeth*. In addition to this, she became one of the few vessels which ran sailings to view the Naval Reviews at Spithead. In fact she is the only vessel to have been present at all seven of these reviews since the Second World War. *Balmoral* has carried both HRH Prince Philip and HRH Princess Anne during her sixty years in service.

By 1968 many excursion steamers and motor vessels operating around the UK coast had gone, but *Balmoral* was to become popular in the Bristol Channel area. Red Funnel had plans for new horizons as car traffic to the Isle of Wight was on the increase. It was sad that until *Waverley* came south ten years later, the popular 'Round the Island' cruise had to go. *Balmoral* remained the property of Red Funnel until 1979, being chartered to P&A Campbell for their services on the Bristol Channel, partnering her erstwhile Red Funnel fleetmate *Vecta* (now sailing as *Westward Ho*) until her withdrawal after the 1971 season.

On the Bristol Channel *Balmoral* offered a variety of sailings, with the timings and destinations changing daily. Because of the wide tidal range there, a regular schedule has never been possible. Sailings ran from Cardiff and Penarth on the Welsh side, and from Bristol, Clevedon and Weston-super-Mare on the south side, down Channel to Ilfracombe and on to Lundy or a Devon Coast cruise, often with calls by tender at Lynmouth or Clovelly. Sailings were also offered from Swansea and Mumbles across to Ilfracombe, and from upchannel piers to Mumbles, around the Gower coast and on occasion to Tenby. Occasional sailings were made as far as Padstow, and weekend trips to the Scilly Isles at the beginning or end of the season. She also acted as a tender to the cruise liners *Kungsholm* and *Gripsholm* on a number of occasions, visiting the North Wales coast and the Isle of Man.

As far as the paddle steamers in the Bristol Channel were concerned, the glory days had gone, but these two vessels, and in particular *Balmoral*, kept the link alive until *Waverley* ventured to the area, firstly in 1979, when there was a first meeting of what were to be Britain's last two surviving coastal excursion steamers at Ilfracombe and Lundy. During her short visit, who would have thought that the Scottish house flag of the Waverley Steam Navigation Company would fly over both vessels? Surely Peter and Alex Campbell, who had moved their eponymous company from the Clyde to the Bristol Channel in 1887, would have been proud.

As a footnote to *Balmoral* in Red Funnel days, we make mention of the many liners which sailed from Southampton. *Balmoral* sailed from Greenock when the last purpose-built transatlantic liner, *Queen Elizabeth 2*, visited Greenock on Sunday 5 October 2008, on her farewell visit to the river of her birth before her retirement to Dubai.

The P&A Campbell Years

In the spring of 1969, P&A Campbell Ltd of Cardiff announced that they had signed a charter agreement with Red Funnel for the use of *Balmoral* on their Bristol Channel services. In effect, she was to be a replacement for the much-loved *Bristol Queen*.

Balmoral had received her winter overhaul at the Cosens & Co. yard at Weymouth, and left that port for Barry on 16 May. The only visible alteration to her former colour scheme was that the funnel was painted white. For the delivery voyage she was under the command of Capt. Jack Wide, who was to be closely identified with her over the next ten years. She arrived at Barry Pier the next day in mid-morning. There then followed a few days of crew familiarisation and storing, and she entered service on 23 May as a White Funnel steamer on the Cardiff to Weston 'ferry' service. On 24 May she made her first trip to Ilfracombe from Penarth, with the then-usual Saturday excursion to Mumbles. This was followed by a very busy period on all the usual Channel long-distance services.

During her first season under the familiar blue and white ball-and-chevron flag of P&A Campbell, *Balmoral* proved very popular with passengers. She was just that bit faster and more comfortable than her running mate MV *Westward Ho*, which had provided the majority of the long-distance sailings on the channel since the demise of the paddle steamers. As the charter of *Balmoral* had been arranged very much at the last minute, her potential was not fully utilised, the timetable used being in the main that which had been devised for *Westward Ho* and the small and slow *St Trillo*. In effect, *Balmoral* took over *Westward Ho's* schedule, and *St Trillo* was despatched to North Wales to give another season of sailings (her last) in that area.

During her time with Campbell's, the former open car-deck aft was retained, and proved very popular with passengers as a sheltered open area – almost a suntrap at times. This space has now, of course, been replaced by the new dining saloon and galley. The catering offered was of the usual hit-and-miss Campbell variety, but waiter service was offered for the first couple of seasons in the dining saloon. At that time, the cafeteria was forward in the area that is today the bar, and this was utilised as the dining saloon. Snacks, teas and coffees were provided in the area that is now the crew mess-room. The present souvenir shop area was a bar, and the splendid art deco bar aft on the lower deck was as it still is today. During the 1969 season, *Balmoral* many times came to the rescue of *Westward Ho*, which was having ever-increasing problems with her ageing engines. The charter of *Balmoral* had proved a great success, and she continued to serve Campbell's reliably for another decade.

At the end of the 1969 season, *Balmoral* sailed back to Weymouth where winter maintenance work was carried out by Cosens & Co., (who were, of course, part of the Red Funnel group).

For the 1970 season, the full potential of *Balmoral* was taken into account in the preparation of the timetables. *St Trillo* had been withdrawn form service at the end of 1969, and regular North Wales services were to be abandoned. The Bristol Channel services were in the hands of *Balmoral* and *Westward Ho*, and the speed of *Balmoral* would enable more old favourite cruises of the paddle-steamer days to be resumed. Memorable sailings in 1970 included a Paddle Steamer Preservation Society charter to Lundy on 5 July, the day that the SS *Great Britain* came home to Bristol. This meant that the sailing had to be commenced from Avonmouth, not Bristol, as the River Avon was closed to all traffic that morning. Later in the season an excellent variety of cruises were operated to port such as Tenby, Padstow, and Clovelly, all now possible again with the speed of *Balmoral*.

During the ensuing ten years, a tremendous variety of sailings took place, taking *Balmoral* to many of the ports which have become familiar to us today. She often acted as a tender to the Swedish America Lines cruise ships which called at British resorts such as Llandudno and Douglas during the 1970s. Often, short public cruises would be offered when *Balmoral* was in the area. In addition, *Bristol Queen's* annual three-day Isles of Scilly trip was revived on a number of occasions, although it has to be said that *Balmoral's* attempts at them were often thwarted by appalling weather!

After a couple of seasons on charter from Red Funnel, *Balmoral* was painted in the full colours of P&A Campbell - the colour scheme she now proudly wears under Waverley Excursions Ltd ownership. Prior to the 1970 season she also acquired a cowl on top of her funnel, so long a feature of the White Funnel paddle steamers.

After the 1971 season, *Westward Ho* was withdrawn and sold due to continuing engine problems. *St Trillo* remained laid up at Barry until she too was sold for scrap in 1973. In 1977, Campbell's acquired the former Isles of Scilly mailship *Scillonian*, and adapted her for use on Bristol Channel services alongside *Balmoral*. She was renamed *Devonia*, and entered service looking very smart in Campbell colours. However, she was not really suitable for the trade, but struggled on for a couple of years before being withdrawn. At the beginning of her Campbell career, she ran unsuccessfully for a few weeks on the Thames.

By the end of the 1970s the writing was well and truly on the wall for the traditional commercially-operated pleasure steamer. European Ferries could see no future in this type of operation, and wished to close down P&A Campbell. Almost entirely due to the efforts of Campbell's managing director, Clifton Smith-Cox, a deal was agreed with the Landmark Trust (the lessees of Lundy) to set up a jointly financed company to operate *Balmoral* in the 1980 season. The new company was known as White Funnel Steamers Ltd, with P&A Campbell as managers of the ship. However, bad weather during the season meant that the number of passengers was low, and the Landmark Trust withdrew from the agreement at the end of the year.

Balmoral under Preservation

Following her last sailing under White Funnel Steamers (supported by the Landmark Trust) in October 1980, many would have thought that it was the end of the great era of 'going for a Channel dap'.

Not so, for the paddle steamer *Waverley* had been triumphantly brought back from the very same end-of-era scenario, up on the Firth of Clyde. Her owners were actively seeking a fleetmate and did so in the autumn of the same year, 1980, with the purchase of the MV *Shanklin*, later to be renamed *Prince Ivanhoe*.

At a meeting in London in December 1980 between *Balmoral's* owners, the Landmark Trust, and Mr J.T. Sylvester of WSN Co., it became very clear that the steamer service on the Bristol Channel was now in the hands of WSN, and destined to be undertaken by the *Prince Ivanhoe* from the summer of 1981 onwards. However, later in that summer she ran aground in Port Eynon on the Gower Coast and was lost, fortunately with no direct loss of life (although one passenger died of a heart attack later on the beach). This brought to an end the bravest of all attempts to keep the memory of the P&A Campbell fleet alive.

The last vestige of the real Campbell era left the Channel in 1982, bound for Dundee and a career as a floating restaurant owned by Craig Inns Ltd. This was, however, a financial failure and closed after only a few months.

Balmoral was sold by the Bank of Scotland to Helseam Ltd, and in March 1985 she steamed through the Pentland Firth to Glasgow and a £300,000 rebuild. The authors pay tribute to Mrs Jennifer Leech, without whom WSN/WEL would be so much worse off. She was also Mrs *Balmoral*, until retirement from both in the early 1990s.

The big refit continued apace and was completed in Govan Dry Dock, Glasgow. Following trials, she arrived at her old and new home port, Bristol, on the late evening of 12 April 1986, to a round of applause from some eager fans.

The Bristol Channel business was open and has been so since MV *Balmoral* returned, supplemented by PS *Waverley* for a month in the spring in most years.

It was most of all a tribute to Campbell's that a lot was salvaged from the bones of their effort. An even bigger acknowledgement goes to WSN/WEL for the incredible variety of schedules including sailing round Britain with calls at ports and piers, first by *Waverley* in 1981-83. *Balmoral's* service since 1986 has given her the title of 'Britain's most widely travelled excursion ship'.

Happy sixtieth birthday, *Balmoral*

Alistair Deayton
Iain Quinn
Patrick Murrell

MV *Balmoral*
Timeline: Ownership and Captains

1949: 27 June	Launched by Mrs C.D. Pinnock, wife of the Red Funnel chairman
1949: 28 October to 3 November	Trials
1949: 13 December	Maiden voyage
1968: 15 September	Final Red Funnel sailing

Captains:

1949 to late **1953**	Capt. A.G. Gattsell
late **1953** to **1962**	Capt. N.E. Larkin
1962 until his death in **1967**	Capt. T. Kane
1967 to **1968**	Capt. J. Bowden
Chief Engineer	Mr McLeod
Purser	Mr Angell

1969: April	Announcement in *Bristol Evening Post* of her transfer on charter to P&A Campbell. Her masters on the Bristol Channel included captains Hardcastle, Wide and Smith
1979	Purchased by P&A Campbell Ltd, by now owned by European Ferries
1979: 19 October	Final sailing for P&A Campbell Ltd
1980: 27 March	A new company, White Funnel Steamers Ltd, jointly owned by P&A Campbell and the Landmark Trust, lessees of the island of Lundy, was formed to charter *Balmoral* from P&A Campbell and operate the excursion programme. Any profits would go towards the island of Lundy
1980: 14 October	Laid up at Bristol at end of season
1980: December	The business was handed over to Waverley Steam Navigation Ltd and the Firth of Clyde Steam Packet Co. in London, with White Funnel as agents
1981: 3 August	The Bristol Channel excursion sailings was left to *Waverley* alone, following the loss of *Prince Ivanhoe*
1982: March	Sold to Craig Inns Ltd of Dundee for use as a floating restaurant. Sailed to Dundee via the English Channel under her own power
1985: 22 February	Purchased for preservation by Waverley Steam Navigation Co. (WSN) and *Balmoral* Restoration Fund
1985: 31 March	Following a brief survey, *Balmoral* sailed back from Dundee to Glasgow via the north of Scotland under her own power
1986: April	Owned by Helseam Ltd, chartered to Waverley Excursions Ltd (WEL), with *Waverley* in partnership with *Balmoral*
1988	Owned by Balmoral Excursions Ltd, chartered to Waverley Excursions Ltd
1992	Owned by Waverley Steam Navigation Ltd, operated by Waverley Excursions Ltd

Captains:

A considerable number of captains have been on her over the past twenty-three years for different periods of time. These have included captains S.P. Michel, D.L. Neill, E.L. Davies, S.P. Colledge, G. Gellatly, A.D. Brian, I. Clarke, P. Tambling, G. Wilson, E.C. Davies and J. Addison.

Timeline: Appearance and Liveries

1949-1968	Red funnel and car deck aft
1954	Stump mainmast replaced by a full-size one
1964	Radar fitted
1969	White funnel, no cowl; car deck not used as such
1970-1980	White funnel with cowl; car deck not used as such
1981-1985	Same livery: promenade deck extended aft. This was not full-length
1985-1986 (winter)	Car deck enclosed to facilitate the construction of a dining saloon. New deck house and purser's office, new foremast and new extended bridge fitted. White hull, yellow funnel
1987-1991	Same livery with green flashings
1992	Hull and boot-topping painted green, in a darker shade than previous boot-topping
1993	Red funnel, thin gold band, black top
1994	Pale yellow funnel, green top and gold band
1995	Full Campbell livery restored
2009	Both masts slightly pruned to allow greater use of the River Wye

At some time since 1986 the foremast has been replaced

Brief trial liveries

1994	Red funnel, thin white band, black top
1994 (Oban spell)	Pale yellow funnel, green top, no band
2001	Red funnel, thin white band, deep black top
2001 (autumn, four days Clyde spell only)	Yellow funnel with deep black top, then red funnel with black top, full brown bridge wings. She sailed Glasgow to Tarbert (Loch Fyne) only, for a charter to BBC Scotland for the *Crowdie and Cream* series. *Balmoral* spent the winter of 2001 to 2002 in these colours at Princes Wharf, Bristol.

Gazetteer of Ports called at by MV *Balmoral* under WSN Preservation (1985 to date)

The South Coast
Bournemouth
Bridport
Eastbourne – Pier
Eastbourne – Royal Sovereign
Folkestone
Littlehampton
Lulworth Cove – tender
Newhaven
Newport (IOW)
Poole
Portsmouth
Ryde
Sandown
Shoreham
Southampton
Southsea
Swanage
Totland Bay
Weymouth
Worthing
Yarmouth (IOW)

The Bristol Channel
Avonmouth
Barry
Barry Island Harbour
Bideford
Bridgwater
Bristol
Briton Ferry
Cardiff
Clevedon
Clovelly – tender
Gloucester
Ilfracombe
Lundy – Pier
Lundy – tender
Lydney
Lynmouth – tender
Milfrod Haven

Minehead
Newport (Mon)
Padstow
Pembroke Dock
Penarth
Porthcawl
Portishead
Sharpness
Steepholm
Swansea
Tenby
Watchet
Weston-super-Mare

Liverpool & North Wales
Blackpool – North Pier
Caernarfon
Ellesmere Port
Holyhead
Liverpool
Llandudno
Menai Bridge
Morecambe
Mostyn
Port Penrhyn
Seacombe

The Irish Sea & Isle of Man
Ballycastle – new
Ballycastle – old
Bangor
Bantry Bay
Barrow
Belfast
Carrickfergus
Castletownbere
Castletownbere – tender
Coleraine
Donaghadee
Douglas
Garlieston

Killyleagh
Kinsale
Larne
Londonderry
Millom
Moville
Newry
Peel
Port Erin
Port St Mary
Portaferry
Ramsey
Rathlin
Red Bay
Warrenpoint
Whitehaven
Workington

The Firth of Clyde
Ardrossan
Arrochar (Succoth)
Ayr
Blairmore
Brodick
Campbeltown
Carrick Castle
Clydebank – river berth
Clydebank – Rothesay Dock
Dunoon – New
Dunoon – Old
Girvan
Glasgow – Anderston Quay
Glasgow – Pacific Quay
Glasgow – Windmillcroft Quay
Glasgow – Yorkhill Basin
Gourock 1A Berth
Gourock
Govan – Dry dock and Basin
Greenock – CHQ
Helensburgh
Kilcreggan

Kilmun
Largs
Lochranza
Millport
Renfrew – Pudzeoch Basin
Rothesay
Sandbank
Tarbert – on charter for BBC
for *Crowdies and Cream*
Tighnabruaich
Wemyss Bay

West Highlands
Canna
Colonsay
Fort William
Gigha
Iona – tender
Kennacraig
Oban – North Pier
Oban – Railway Pier
Port Askaig
Port Ellen
Tobermory

North & East Coasts of Scotland
Aberdeen
Aberdour
Anstruther
Banff
Bo'ness
Burntisland
Dundee
Eyemouth
Fraserburgh
Grangemouth
Granton
Invergordon
Inverness
Leith
Macduff
Montrose
Perth
Rosyth Naval Dockyard

Scrabster
St Andrews
Stonehaven
Wick

East Coast of England
Amble
Berwick
Blyth
Goole
Grimsby
Hartlepool
Hull
Ipswich
Keadby
Middlesbrough
Newcastle
North Shields
Scarborough
Sunderland
Whitby

Thames & Medway
Brighlingsea
Clacton
Colchester
Great Yarmouth
Harwich
London – Tower Pier
London – London Bridge City
   Pier
London – Masthouse Terrace
   Pier
Margate
Greenwich – Millennium Pier
PS *Kingswear Castle* – tender
Ramsgate
Rochester
Southend
Strood
Tilbury
Walton-on-the-Naze
Whitstable
Wivenhoe
Woolwich

Special Calls
Aberdyfi
Brighton
Boulogne
Calais
Lamlash
Ormidale
Penzance
RMS *Queen Elizabeth* 2
   – tender to
Rotterdam
Scilly Isles – on charter for
   Scillonian III
St Ives

Chapter 1: The South Coast & Isle of Wight

Balmoral operated in this area from 1949 until 1968, and was very much the flagship of the island services from Southampton. Under the WSN flag she can only operate to the limited piers to the north of the island, at Ryde and Yarmouth, but she has sailed further into the heart of Wight than any other steamer, venturing up the Medina to Newport. From Penzance to Rye, few piers and harbours have not seen the ship. Furthermore, on all the cruises *Balmoral* sails, she gives an unrivalled view of the coast for her passengers, the stunning views of Dorset's Jurassic coast, between Swanage and Lulworth Cove, being a fine example.

An official card showing the paddle steamer *Balmoral*, with the company crest above, and vignettes of Southampton, Brighton, the Isle of Wight and Bournemouth in the four corners.

Balmoral was the second vessel of that name in the Southampton, Isle of Wight and South of England Royal Mail Steam Packet Co.'s fleet. The first was this paddle steamer, built in 1900 by McKnight of Ayr, with compound engines by Hutson & Co. of Glasgow. She was the flagship of the fleet, and was employed both on cross-channel excursions to Cherbourg and coastal trips to Eastbourne, Brighton, Weymouth and Torquay. She served in the First World War, initially for three months as a troopship, and then as a minesweeper. In the Second World War she sailed as an auxiliary anti-aircraft ship, and later as an accommodation ship. At the end of that war she was in very poor condition, and was not deemed worthy of refurbishment, being scrapped in 1949.

Balmoral was really a replacement for the paddle steamer *Gracie Fields*, built in 1936 by J.I. Thornycroft at Woolston, and fitted with a car deck forward. She had been sunk after being hit by a bomb whilst evacuating troops from Dunkirk on 30 May 1940.

When she entered service, *Balmoral* replaced *Princess Helena* on the Southampton to Cowes service. She had been built as far back as 1885 by Barclay Curle's in Glasgow. She spent her final operational years on the car-ferry service, and was scrapped in 1952 after three years in reserve.

Balmoral was the third in a series of similar twin-screw motor vessels built for Red Funnel. The first was *Medina*, built in 1931 by Thornycroft. She was withdrawn in 1962 and was sold for use at Gibraltar, where she was renamed *Mons Abyla*, returning to the UK in 1972. Thereafter she spent twenty-five years in a peripatetic existence in various static roles around the English coast, interspersed with long periods laid up.

The second of the three motor vessels was *Vecta*, built in 1938 with diesel-electric propulsion and Voith-Schneider propellers, which were replaced by normal propellers during the war as spare parts were unavailable. There was a small car deck on the main deck forward, as seen by the windowless openings in this photo. In 1965 she was sold to P&A Campbell, and served on the Bristol Channel under the name *Westward Ho* until 1971. She was then used from 1972 to 1985 as a floating restaurant at Manchester and, after several years laid up, was finally scrapped in 1996. She is seen here approaching Cowes on Easter Sunday, 9 April 1950.

Vecta is seen centrally in this 7 March 1965 view of Southampton Royal Pier, the company headquarters, with *Balmoral* to the left and the car ferry *Carisbrooke Castle* (1959) to the right.

P.S. "Lord Elgin"—Red Funnel Cargo Steamer

DAILY CARGO SERVICE
between
SOUTHAMPTON & COWES

Every week-day throughout the year (Bank Holidays excepted) the Red Funnel Steamer "Lord Elgin" operates a Cargo Service to and from the Isle of Wight *via* the above ports. Merchandise of every description is accepted for transport, facilities for the loading and handling of livestock and unusual cargoes being available at either terminal.

Intending consignors should apply to
The General Manager,
Southampton, Isle of Wight and South of England Royal
Mail Steam Packet Company Limited.
Western Esplanade,   'Phone: 6571-2.
SOUTHAMPTON.   'Grams: "Siwepaco," So'ton.
or to the LOCAL MANAGER of the above Company.
Fountain Pier, Cowes, I.W.   'Phone: Cowes 16.
124

Up until September 1952 a cargo service to Cowes was maintained, alongside the *Balmoral*, by the venerable *Lord Elgin*, which dated back to 1876 and had originally run on the Firth of Forth. She continued operating the cargo run when her replacement was off for overhaul until May 1955.

An official Red Funnel postcard of *Balmoral* in her early condition with a stump mainmast.

SOUTHAMPTON-ISLE OF WIGHT

THE
RED FUNNEL
ROUTE

to

WEST COWES
and
EAST COWES

for

PASSENGERS
MOTOR CARS
COMMERCIAL VEHICLES

SOUTHAMPTON
ROYAL PIER

WEST
COWES

EAST
COWES

RYDE

YARMOUTH

NEWPORT

FRESHWATER

SANDOWN

SHANKLIN

VENTNOR

The Red Funnel map from their 1966 brochure for the Cowes service.

Balmoral moored at Southampton, Royal Pier, on 9 April 1950.

Full astern out of Ventnor, 11 August 1953. Ventnor is one of the Isle of Wight piers that has been lost to the present generation, the landing stage having been partially removed in 1967 and the pier demolished in 1993.

Balmoral on 27 June 1967 in her Red Funnel condition.

Balmoral in Southampton Water, heading homewards on 17 June 1967, flying the company house flag.

The company house flag representing the colours of the company's first four steamers, *Pearl, Ruby, Emerald* and *Sapphire*.

The Red Funnel excursion programme for August 1959, headed by a drawing of *Balmoral*, showing trips from Southampton to Ryde, Southsea, Sandown and Shanklin every day except Fridays, extended to Ventnor on some Mondays and on Wednesdays, and to Ventnor and round the island on Tuesdays and Thursdays. Additional trips were offered to Ryde, only these excursions possibly then offering a trip to Southampton to see the liners. There were no sailings on Saturdays, that being the busy day on the Cowes service. At this time Red Funnel had three vessels available for excursions, *Medina, Vecta* and *Balmoral*.

In 1961 *Balmoral* was still used to advertise the ferry service to Cowes, although some sailings were then undertaken by *Carisbrooke Castle*. The following year the second car ferry, *Osborne Castle*, entered service, and *Balmoral* was relegated to the excursion services.

A programme for August 1966 showing excursions form the four Isle of Wight piers – Ryde, Sandown, Shanklin and Ventnor – including trips to Southampton Docks to see *Queen Mary* or *Queen Elizabeth*. By this time *Balmoral* was carrying out the excursion programme alone. May and June of that year had seen the seamen's strike, when the Cunard Queens and many other liners were laid up at Southampton for six weeks.

RED FUNNEL STEAMERS

PASSENGER AND VEHICLE SERVICE

BETWEEN

SOUTHAMPTON AND WEST AND EAST COWES

UNTIL 22nd SEPTEMBER, 1968

AND

EXCURSION PROGRAMME

1st AUGUST to 31st AUGUST, 1968

REFRESHMENT FACILITIES AVAILABLE ABOARD ALL VESSELS

THE ABOVE SERVICES AND EXCURSIONS ARE LIABLE TO ALTERATION AT SHORT NOTICE AND THE TIME OF ARRIVAL MAY VARY, BEING SUBJECT TO WEATHER AND/OR OTHER CONDITIONS OUTSIDE THE CONTROL OF THE COMPANY

The Southampton excursion programme for August 1968, *Balmoral's* last season for Red Funnel.

RED FUNNEL STEAMERS

SEE THE ISLE OF WIGHT FROM THE OUTSIDE!

View the wonderful coastline from the sea—Bembridge—Culver Cliff — Sandown — Shanklin — Dunnose Head — Ventnor — the Undercliff — St. Catherine's Point and Lighthouse — Freshwater Bay — Tennyson Down — the Needles and Lighthouse—Alum Bay (with its coloured cliffs)—Totland Bay—the quaint old harbour of Yarmouth—Cowes (between here and Ryde large liners using the port of Southampton are often seen).

HAVE YOU SEEN THE WORLD'S LARGEST LINERS AT CLOSE QUARTERS OR UNDERWAY?

FOR DETAILS OF SAILINGS EMBRACING THESE ATTRACTIONS AND OTHER DELIGHTFUL CRUISES FROM

RYDE PIER

SEE PROGRAMME INSIDE . . .

1st August to 18th August, 1966

(Weather and other circumstances permitting)

EXCELLENT REFRESHMENT FACILITIES ARE AVAILABLE ON BOARD AND COMMENTARIES ON POINTS OF INTEREST ARE GIVEN EN ROUTE OVER THE PUBLIC ADDRESS SYSTEM.

In 1966 a smaller programme was also available for the excursions from Ryde, the cover of which is seen here.

Balmoral at Sandown Pier, Isle of Wight, on 27 June 1967.

A Red Funnel paper napkin showing a profile of *Balmoral*.

In winter lay-up at Weymouth in the 1965/66 winter, where she was lying adjacent to the paddle steamers *Embassy* and *Princess Elizabeth*.

At Ryde, Isle of Wight, from the Portsmouth ferry *Southsea* or *Brading*.

Off the Isle of Wight, making a sharp turn, flying the P&A Campbell and Red Funnel house flags.

At an unusual call at Newport, Isle of Wight, on 6 June 1992, on a sailing from Swanage, Bournemouth and Yarmouth. She is the only pleasure steamer ever to have called there.

Approaching the pier at Yarmouth, Isle of Wight.

At Yarmouth, with PS *Waverley* and a Wightlink 'C'-class car ferry arriving from Lymington in 1989. This was the first visit of the company's steamers to Yarmouth.

At her overnight berth at Poole Quay with the pleasure launch *Maid of the Harbour.*

A June 2008 leaflet showing *Balmoral* at Lulworth Cove and details of sailings from Weymouth, Bournemouth, Bridport (West Bay), and Yarmouth, Isle of Wight.

Discover

the Coast & Towns of the ISLE of WIGHT - sail all the way to London & see TOWER BRIDGE open just for you - aboard Historic Ship BALMORAL

CRUISES FROM SUSSEX

Welcome Aboard the Historic Ship BALMORAL in 2008 - and Sail Away on an enchanting & exciting cruise. On board - stroll round the promenade sun decks , enjoy a meal or snack in the self-service restaurant; relax in the restored period lounges & bars or visit the souvenir shop for that special memento of your day. BALMORAL is owned by a Charity & British Registered for 683 passengers. There are special fares for Children and Senior Citizens so BOOK NOW and enjoy a great trip for all the family!

from WORTHING Pier

NEEDLES & LIGHTHOUSE

SUNDAY JUNE 22 Leave 1pm back 9.30pm
Sail through the Solent to visit charming Yarmouth - Isle of Wight £26.95 SENIOR CITIZENS £24.95 Or stay aboard for the full cruise viewing the famous Needles & Lighthouse £29.95 SC £27.95. *In the evening sail into Portsmouth Harbour to join your coach for the return journey.*

from EASTBOURNE Royal Sovereign

Passengers park in Waterfront Car Park opp the Sovereign Harbour Yacht Club.
Assembly by the blue gates opp the Sovereign Harbour Yacht Club where shuttle bus takes you to the RNLI Station opp Lock 2 to board Balmoral.

NEEDLES & LIGHTHOUSE

SUNDAY JUNE 22 Leave 11am back 10pm
Join an inclusive coach to board Balmoral at Worthing Pier and sail to Isle of Wight and visit Yarmouth £27.95 SENIOR CITIZENS £25.95 Or stay aboard for the full cruise along the dramatic coastline of the Isle of Wight to the Needles – see the towering cliffs, seabirds & lighthouse £29.95 SC £27.95 In the evening - see ships of the Royal Navy & HMS Warrior as you sail into Portsmouth Harbour to join your coach for the return journey to Eastbourne.

SAIL THROUGH TOWER BRIDGE

WEDNESDAY JUNE 25 Leave 9am back 9.30pm
Day Cruise to London – sail round Dungeness - North Foreland – and cruise up the Thames to the heart of London. See Thames Flood Barrier - magnificent Greenwich Waterfront – Millennium Dome – Canary Wharf & see Tower Bridge open for you to sail through. With views of Tower of London & HMS Belfast join your inclusive coach home £39.95 SC £37.95.

from RYE Wharf

Free Car Parking at Rye Harbour Car Park- Allow 10 mins to walk to Wharf

SAIL THROUGH TOWER BRIDGE

MONDAY JUNE 30 Leave 8.30am back 9.30pm
Don't miss the only sailing from Rye aboard Balmoral in 2008. Magnificent Day Cruise to London – sail round Dungeness - North Foreland – and cruise up the Thames to the heart of London. See Thames Flood Barrier - magnificent Greenwich Waterfront – Millennium Dome – Canary Wharf & see Tower Bridge open for you to sail through. With views of Tower of London & HMS Belfast you join your inclusive coach for Rye £39.95 SENIOR CITIZENS £37.95.

CHILDREN Half Fare - Under 5s Travel FREE

Discounts for Groups of 10 and more - Call Sharon on 0845 130 4647 or email sharon@waverleyexcursions.co.uk

BE SURE OF YOUR TICKETS CALL 0845 130 4647

Buy Tickets from Tourist Information Centres at Bournemouth, Weymouth, Ringwood, Hayling Island, Christchurch, Wimborne, Bridport & all Isle of Wight Tourist Information Centres.

OR BUY YOUR TICKETS ON BOARD WHEN YOU SAIL

Find Out More & Book Online www.waverleyexcursions.co.uk

Details of 2008 sailings westbound from Worthing and Eastbourne, round to the River Thames and through Tower Bridge from Eastbourne and Rye.

Chapter 2: The Bristol Channel

This area brings *Balmoral* into her second home, the area which she has served for the longest period in her sixty years, with a total of twelve years under the P&A Campbell flag and twenty-three years under the WSN flag. The much-loved Bristol Channel is the start and finish of all her annual timetables. She lays up for the winter in Bristol at Princes Wharf, where her loyal band of volunteers get dirty bringing the ship up to standard – 'all shipshape and Bristol fashion' – for the following season. From 1969 to date *Balmoral* has cruised the entire length and breadth of this area. She has only missed the years 1981-85 inclusive. This is a very vulnerable part of her schedule because of its exposure to almost all directions of wind. Again, *Balmoral* provides unparalleled views of these real deep-sea coastal waters.

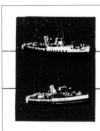

P & A Campbell Ltd
PASSENGER SHIP OWNERS

4 DOCK CHAMBERS   BUTE STREET   CARDIFF   TEL CARDIFF 20255

Please address all replies to: Traffic Manager.

2.6.70

The P&A Campbell letter heading used in 1970 showing *Balmoral* and *Westward Ho*.

The P&A Campbell house flag.

Vecta in the River Avon on her first trip from Bristol for P&A Campbell, 25 September 1965. She had an engine overhaul at Weymouth over the ensuing winter, and emerged for the 1966 season renamed *Westward Ho* (without the exclamation mark carried by the Devon village and the novel by Charles Kingsley).

Balmoral arrived in the P&A Campbell fleet to replace the paddle steamer *Bristol Queen*, seen here in the River Avon in the early 1960s.

Balmoral, *Westward Ho*, and *St Trillo* in winter lay up at Barry Dock in December 1970. *St Trillo* was never to sail again, and *Westward Ho* only had one more season's service.

Balmoral meets *Westward Ho* at Ilfracombe in her second month on the Bristol Channel, June 1969.

A choppy day in the Bristol Channel, 25 August 1969.

WHITE FUNNEL FLEET

Sailings from HOTWELLS LANDING STAGE, BRISTOL

by the Motor Vessels BALMORAL & WESTWARD HO

THE VESSELS of the White Funnel Fleet are large sea-going ships capable of accommodating up to 850 passengers. The vessels have a restaurant and tea bar where meals and snacks can be obtained, also fully licensed bars. There are sun lounges, spacious open decks and covered accommodation is available sufficient for all passengers.

(Also Combined Coach and Steamer Trips from Canons Marsh Coach Park)

On certain occasions as set out below, the steamer departs from and returns to Hotwells Landing Stage which is situated almost under the Suspension Bridge. On some days the steamer departs from Hotwells Landing Stage but returns to Weston whence passengers are conveyed by coach to Bristol. On certain further occasions, passengers travel from Bristol (Canons Marsh Coach Park) by coach to Weston thence by steamer and return to Hotwells Landing Stage. The details of all the foregoing services are given below.

On many occasions passengers are conveyed from Canons Marsh Coach Park by motor coach either to Weston or Clevedon to connect with steamers leaving those resorts. On return to either Weston or Clevedon, passengers are met at their respective piers and brought back to Canons Marsh Coach Park. Where this service operates, the coaches leave Canons Marsh Coach Park 1½ hours before the departure of the steamer at Weston, or 1 hour before the departure from Clevedon. On return the coach reaches Canons Marsh Coach Park about 1½ hours after the steamer arrives at Weston or 1 hour after the steamer arrives at Clevedon. On these occasions departure times from Canons Marsh Coach Park together with details of the arrival times at destinations, the return times from destinations and the arrival time back at Bristol are given below.

Passengers are asked when planning an excursion to note carefully whether they leave Bristol by steamer from Hotwells Landing Stage or by coach from Canons Marsh Coach Park.

It is not necessary to make advance bookings for any excursions, but these may be made if desired.

The 1969 handbill for sailings from Bristol (Hotwells Landing Stage). For 1969 P&A Campbell used a drawing of *St Trillo* to headline their publicity.

WHITE FUNNEL FLEET

Sailings from CARDIFF (Pier Head) PENARTH & BARRY PIERS

by the Motor Vessels BALMORAL & WESTWARD HO

THE VESSELS of the White Funnel Fleet are large sea-going ships capable of accommodating up to 850 passengers. The vessels have a restaurant and tea bar where meals and snacks can be obtained, also fully licensed bars. There are sun lounges, spacious open decks and covered accommodation is available sufficient for all passengers.

The header for the 1969 season's sailings from Cardiff, the headquarters of the company, as well as Penarth and Barry piers.

WHITE FUNNEL FLEET

Sailings from THE HARBOUR, LYNMOUTH
by the Motor Vessels BALMORAL & WESTWARD HO

THE VESSELS of the White Funnel Fleet are large sea-going ships capable of accommodating up to 850 passengers. The vessels have a restaurant and tea bar where meals and snacks can be obtained, also fully licensed bars. There are sun lounges, spacious open decks and covered accommodation is available sufficient for all passengers.

SEASON 1969

TUESDAY, MAY 27th
12.15 p.m. Return Trip to ILFRACOMBE. Leave Ilfracombe 2.20 p.m., due Lynmouth about 3.20 p.m. Fare 13/6d.
12.15 p.m. Circular Trip to ILFRACOMBE. Returning from Ilfracombe (Bus Station) by the Southern National Omnibus Co. Ltd. at 2.5 p.m. Combined Fare 13/6d.
3.10 p.m. Afternoon Cruise along the COASTS of DEVON and SOMERSET, passing the Foreland Point and Lighthouse, Glenthorne, etc., and to Porlock Bay. Back about 5.10 p.m. Fare 11/-.
6.50 p.m. Single Trip to ILFRACOMBE and MUMBLES.
Note: Steamer leaves Mumbles 9.20 a.m., Ilfracombe 11.30 a.m., due Lynmouth about 12.25 p.m.

TUESDAY, JUNE 3rd
11.30 a.m. To LUNDY ISLAND (to land). Leave Lundy Island 4.20 p.m., due Lynmouth about 7.5 p.m. Day Return Fare 30/-.
11.30 a.m. Return Trip to ILFRACOMBE. Leave Ilfracombe 6.10 p.m., due Lynmouth about 7.5 p.m. Fare 13/6d.
11.30 a.m. Circular Trip to ILFRACOMBE. Returning from Ilfracombe (Bus Station) by the Southern National Omnibus Co. Ltd. at 2.5 p.m. Combined Fare 13/6d.
6.50 p.m. Single Trip to MINEHEAD, BARRY, PENARTH and CARDIFF.
Note: Steamer leaves Cardiff 8.20 a.m., Penarth 8.30 a.m., Barry 9.15 a.m., Minehead 10.35 a.m., due Lynmouth about 11.45 a.m.

THURSDAY, JUNE 19th
11.25 a.m. To LUNDY ISLAND (to land). Leave Lundy Island 4.25 p.m., due Lynmouth about 7.30 p.m. Day Return Fare 30/-.
11.25 a.m. Return Trip to ILFRACOMBE. Leave Ilfracombe 6.35 p.m., due Lynmouth about 7.30 p.m. Fare 13/6d.
11.25 a.m. Circular Trip to ILFRACOMBE. Returning from Ilfracombe (Bus Station) by the Southern National Omnibus Co. Ltd. at 2.5 p.m., 3.35 p.m., 5.50 p.m. and 6.35 p.m. Combined Fare 13/6d.
7.15 p.m. Single Trip to MINEHEAD, BARRY, PENARTH and CARDIFF.
Note: Steamer leaves Cardiff 8.30 a.m., Penarth 8.40 a.m., Barry 9.20 a.m., Minehead 10.35 a.m., due Lynmouth about 11.40 a.m.

SUNDAY, JUNE 22nd
12.20 p.m. To LUNDY ISLAND (to land). Leave Lundy Island 5.10 p.m., due Lynmouth about 7.55 p.m. Day Return Fare 30/-.
12.20 p.m. Return Trip to ILFRACOMBE. Leave Ilfracombe 7.0 p.m., due Lynmouth about 7.55 p.m. Fare 13/6d.
12.20 p.m. Circular Trip to ILFRACOMBE. Returning from Ilfracombe (Bus Station) by the Southern National Omnibus Co. Ltd. at 2.35 p.m., 4.5 p.m., 5.50 p.m. and 7.20 p.m. Combined Fare 13/6d.
7.40 p.m. Single Trip to BARRY, PENARTH and CARDIFF.
Note: Steamer leaves Cardiff 7.20 a.m., Penarth 9.30 a.m., Barry 10.10 a.m., Minehead 11.20 a.m., due Lynmouth about 12.35 p.m.

TUESDAY, JUNE 24th
11.25 a.m. To LUNDY ISLAND (to land). Leave Lundy Island 4.20 p.m., due Lynmouth about 7.30 p.m. Fare 13/6d.
11.25 a.m. Return Trip to ILFRACOMBE. Leave Ilfracombe 6.15 p.m., due Lynmouth about 7.30 p.m. Fare 13/6d.
11.25 a.m. Circular Trip to ILFRACOMBE. Returning from Lynton (Bus Station) by the Southern National Omnibus Co. Ltd. at 2.5 p.m., 3.35 p.m., 5.5 p.m. and 6.35 p.m. Combined Fare 13/6d.
6.55 p.m. Single Trip to BARRY (and train to CARDIFF).
Note: Steamer leaves Barry 9.0 a.m., due Lynmouth about 11.40 a.m.

WEDNESDAY, JULY 2nd
11.30 a.m. To LUNDY ISLAND (to land). Leave Lundy Island 4.25 p.m., due Lynmouth about 7.10 p.m. Day Return Fare 30/-.
11.30 a.m. Return Trip to ILFRACOMBE. Leave Ilfracombe 6.15 p.m., due Lynmouth about 7.10 p.m. Fare 13/6d.
11.30 a.m. Circular Trip to ILFRACOMBE. Returning from Ilfracombe (Bus Station) by the Southern National Omnibus Co. Ltd. at 2.5 p.m., 3.35 p.m., 5.5 p.m. and 6.35 p.m. Combined Fare 13/6d.
6.55 p.m. Single Trip to MINEHEAD, BARRY, PENARTH and CARDIFF.
Note: Steamer leaves Cardiff 8.45 a.m., Penarth 8.55 a.m., Barry 9.35 a.m., Minehead 10.45 a.m., due Lynmouth about 11.45 a.m.

TUESDAY, JULY 8th
11.5 a.m. To LUNDY ISLAND (to land). Leave Lundy Island 4.20 p.m., due Lynmouth about 7.10 p.m. Day Return Fare 30/-.
11.5 a.m. Return Trip to ILFRACOMBE. Leave Ilfracombe 6.15 p.m., due Lynmouth about 7.10 p.m. Fare 13/6d.
11.5 a.m. Circular Trip to ILFRACOMBE. Returning from Ilfracombe (Bus Station) by the Southern National Omnibus Co. Ltd. at 2.5 p.m. Combined Fare 13/6d.
6.55 p.m. Single Trip to BARRY (and train to CARDIFF).
Note: Steamer leaves Barry 9.0 a.m., due Lynmouth about 11.20 a.m.

TUESDAY, JULY 15th
12.30 p.m. Return Trip to ILFRACOMBE. Leave Ilfracombe 2.20 p.m., due Lynmouth about 3.20 p.m.
12.30 p.m. Circular Trip to ILFRACOMBE. Returning from Ilfracombe (Bus Station) by the Southern National Omnibus Co. Ltd. at 2.5 p.m., 3.35 p.m., 5.5 p.m. and 6.35 p.m. Combined Fare 13/6d.
3.15 p.m. Afternoon Cruise along the COASTS of DEVON and SOMERSET, passing the Foreland Point and Lighthouse, Glenthorne, etc., and to Porlock Bay. Back about 5.10 p.m. Fare 11/-.
Note: Steamer leaves Swansea 9.0 a.m., Mumbles 9.25 a.m., Ilfracombe 11.35 a.m., due Lynmouth 12.30 p.m.

THURSDAY, JULY 17th
11.25 a.m. To LUNDY ISLAND (to land). Leave Lundy Island 4.20 p.m., due Lynmouth about 7.10 p.m. Day Return Fare 30/-.
11.25 a.m. Return Trip to ILFRACOMBE. Leave Ilfracombe 6.15 p.m., due Lynmouth about 7.10 p.m. Fare 13/6d.
11.25 a.m. Circular Trip to ILFRACOMBE. Returning from Ilfracombe (Bus Station) by the Southern National Omnibus Co. Ltd. at 2.5 p.m., 3.35 p.m., 5.5 p.m. and 6.35 p.m. Combined Fare 13/6d.
6.55 p.m. Single Trip to MINEHEAD, BARRY, PENARTH and CARDIFF.
Note: Steamer leaves Cardiff 8.25 a.m., Penarth 8.35 a.m., Barry 9.15 a.m., Minehead 10.30 a.m., due Lynmouth about 11.40 a.m.

TUESDAY, JULY 22nd
11.30 a.m. To LUNDY ISLAND (to land). Leave Lundy Island 4.25 p.m., due Lynmouth about 7.25 p.m. Day Return Fare 30/-.
11.30 a.m. Return Trip to ILFRACOMBE. Leave Ilfracombe 6.30 p.m., due Lynmouth about 7.25 p.m. Fare 13/6d.
11.30 a.m. Circular Trip to ILFRACOMBE. Returning from Ilfracombe (Bus Station) by the Southern National Omnibus Co. Ltd. at 2.5 p.m., 3.35 p.m., 5.5 p.m. and 6.35 p.m. Combined Fare 13/6d.
7.10 p.m. Single Trip to BARRY and CARDIFF.
Note: Steamer leaves Barry 9.15 a.m., Minehead 10.35 a.m., due Lynmouth about 11.45 a.m.

THURSDAY, JULY 24th
12.35 p.m. Return Trip to ILFRACOMBE. Leave Ilfracombe 2.20 p.m.
12.35 p.m. Circular Trips to ILFRACOMBE. Returning from Ilfracombe (Bus Station) by the Southern National Omnibus Co. Ltd. at 2.5 p.m., 3.35 p.m., 5.5 p.m. and 6.35 p.m. Combined Fare 13/6d.

FOR FURTHER SAILINGS, FARES, GENERAL INFORMATION AND CONDITIONS—see over

A 1969 handbill for P&A Campbell sailings from Lynmouth for the first part of the season. Lynmouth is normally thought of as a destination rather than an embarkation point, but quite a variety of sailings was offered from there. These were mainly to Ilfracombe, with occasional trips to Lundy and one-way sailings to Minehead.

WHITE FUNNEL FLEET

SEASON 1969

SPECIAL SHORT CRUISES

from

BARRY PIER

(SEE MAP ON BACK PAGE)

A 1969 leaflet offering short cruises from Barry Pier. Page two lists cruises to such destinations as Breaksea Lightship, Clevedon & Bristol (one-way), the Welsh Coast and Weston & Cardiff. Page three lists trips to Weston, and the back page is a street plan of Barry, showing directions to the harbour.

For details of all regular daily sailings from Cardiff, Penarth and Barry to Weston, Ilfracombe and other resorts see special Handbills.

Visitors at Butlin's Camp at Barry may book for all steamer trips at the Camp Administration Office.

Balmoral at Hotwells Landing Stage, Bristol, on 16 July 1969, during her first Bristol Channel season.

Heading downstream under the Clifton Suspension Bridge, 14 May 1977.

A classic view of *Balmoral* in the River Avon, 14 May 1977.

Balmoral on charter to the RNLI in May 1974, berthed in central Bristol, outside where the Arnolfini Arts Centre now stands and across from where MacBrayne's *Lochiel* lay for many years as a floating pub.

A handbill for the weekend sailing to Penzance and the Isles of Scilly, from 22 to 24 May 1971, from Cardiff, Weston, Ilfracombe and Padstow, with Saturday and Sunday nights spent in Penzance. Another sailing was advertised from 7 to 9 October 1972, this time to St Ives and the Isles of Scilly. Both were advertised by *Balmoral*, although the header still showed the now withdrawn *St Trillo*.

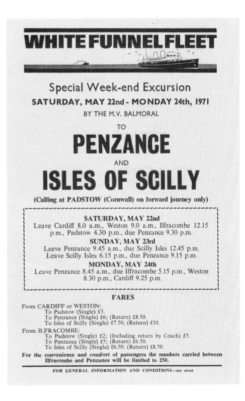

WHITE FUNNEL FLEET

Special Week-end Excursion
SATURDAY, MAY 22nd - MONDAY 24th, 1971
BY THE M.V. BALMORAL
TO

PENZANCE
AND

ISLES OF SCILLY

(Calling at PADSTOW (Cornwall) on forward journey only)

> **SATURDAY, MAY 22nd**
> Leave Cardiff 8.0 a.m., Weston 9.0 a.m., Ilfracombe 12.15 p.m., Padstow 4.30 p.m., due Penzance 9.30 p.m.
> **SUNDAY, MAY 23rd**
> Leave Penzance 9.45 a.m., due Scilly Isles 12.45 p.m.
> Leave Scilly Isles 6.15 p.m., due Penzance 9.15 p.m.
> **MONDAY, MAY 24th**
> Leave Penzance 8.45 a.m., due Ilfracombe 5.15 p.m., Weston 8.30 p.m., Cardiff 9.25 p.m.

FARES

From CARDIFF or WESTON:
    To Padstow (Single) £3.
    To Penzance (Single) £6; (Return) £8.50.
    To Isles of Scilly (Single) £7.50; (Return) £10.
From ILFRACOMBE:
    To Padstow (Single) £2; (Including return by Coach) £3.
    To Penzance (Single) £5; (Return) £6.50.
    To Isles of Scilly (Single) £6.50; (Return) £8.50.
For the convenience and comfort of passengers the numbers carried between Ilfracombe and Penzance will be limited to 250.

FOR GENERAL INFORMATION AND CONDITIONS—see over

WHITE FUNNEL FLEET

Sailings from
SWANSEA (FERRYPORT TERMINAL) and MUMBLES PIER
by the Motor Vessel BALMORAL

MAY 23rd until JULY 31st, 1973

Part of the large handbill showing sailings from Swansea and Mumbles from 23 May to 31 July 1971, showing a drawing of *St Trillo* with the aft funnel removed in the header. This was meant to represent *Balmoral* and *Westward Ho*, but looked more like *St Trillo*'s erstwhile fleet-mate *St Tudno*.

The Ilfracombe handbill for 27 May to 2 July 1978.

WHITE FUNNEL FLEET
P. & A. CAMPBELL LTD.

Sailings from THE PIER, ILFRACOMBE
by the Motor Vessel BALMORAL

SATURDAY, MAY 27th until SUNDAY, JULY 2nd 1978

DAY TRIPS TO LUNDY ISLAND (to land)

Average passage is 1 hour and 40 minutes in each direction

Every TUESDAY, THURSDAY and SUNDAY, also SATURDAY, June 24th

Day Return Fare £4.90, Children half-price

	Leave Ilfracombe	Leave Lundy Island		Leave Ilfracombe	Leave Lundy Island
Sunday, May 28	11.45 a.m.	4.30 p.m.	Sunday, June 18	11.45 a.m.	4.30 p.m.
Tuesday, May 30	11.45 a.m.	4.35 p.m.	Tuesday, June 20	11.45 a.m.	4.35 p.m.
Thursday, June 1	11.45 a.m.	4.35 p.m.	Thursday, June 22	11.45 a.m.	4.35 p.m.
Sunday, June 4	11.45 a.m.	4.30 p.m.	Saturday, June 24	12.35 p.m.	5.00 p.m.
Tuesday, June 6	11.45 a.m.	4.35 p.m.	Sunday, June 25	1.00 p.m.	5.00 p.m.
Thursday, June 8	12.20 p.m.	4.50 p.m.	Tuesday, June 27	11.45 a.m.	4.35 p.m.
Sunday, June 11	1.00 p.m.	5.00 p.m.	Thursday, June 29	11.45 a.m.	4.35 p.m.
Tuesday, June 13	12.20 p.m.	4.50 p.m.	Sunday, July 2	11.45 a.m.	4.30 p.m.
Thursday, June 15	11.45 a.m.	4.35 p.m.			

OTHER EXCURSIONS AND CRUISES

EVERY WEDNESDAY

11.45 a.m. **Day Trip to LYNMOUTH.** Leave Lynmouth 4.45 p.m., due Ilfracombe about 6 p.m. Fare £2.50.

11.45 a.m. **Circular Trip to LYNMOUTH.** Returning from Lynton Bus Station by the Western National Omnibus Co. Ltd., at 5.00 p.m. and 6.30 p.m. Combined Fare £2.50.

11.45 a.m. **Morning Cruise along the North Devon Coast,** passing Hillsborough Hill, Hele Bay, Watermouth Castle and Harbour, Combe Martin, Hangman Hills, Heddonsmouth, Wooda Bay, Castle Rock, etc., and to off **Lynmouth,** back about 2.00 p.m. Fare £1.70.

2.30 p.m. **Afternoon Cruise along the Coasts of Devon and Somerset,** passing Hillsborough Hill, Hele Bay, Watermouth Castle and Harbour, Combe Martin, Hangman Hills, Heddonsmouth, Wooda Bay, Castle Rock, Lynton and Lynmouth, the Foreland Point and Lighthouse, Glenthorne, etc., and towards Porlock Bay, calling off **Lynmouth,** back about 6.00 p.m. Fare £2.20.

A small handbill for evening cruises by *Devonia* (ex-*Scillonian*) for Bristol Wine Festival, 24 & 25 July 1978, from Prince's Wharf and Cumberland Basin, Bristol. Prince's Wharf is *Balmoral*'s winter lay-up berth.

The handbill for sailings from Penarth in 1979, showing the sailings by *Waverley* in her first season on the channel.

On her first call at Tenby, 24 August 1969

At Weston-super-Mare Birnbeck Pier in 1979, having returned from a day trip to Ilfracombe and Lundy.

Approaching Minehead, on 10 May 1980.

A small handbill for an afternoon cruises from
Minehead to Porlock Bat on 16 August 1978

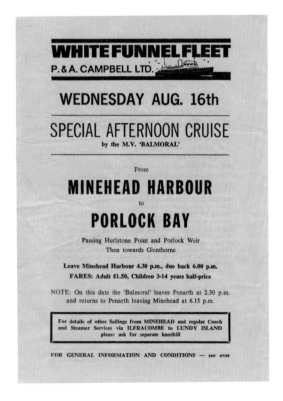

WHITE FUNNEL FLEET
P. & A. CAMPBELL LTD.

Sailings from

PENARTH PIER

Early Season Sailings
(including Easter Holidays)

Easter Monday, April 16th until May 20th 1979

EASTER MONDAY, APRIL 16th
(Bank Holiday)
WESTON. Leave Penarth 10.15 a.m. Leave Weston 8.30 p.m.
10.15 a.m. Day Trip to ILFRACOMBE and Cruise to BAGGY POINT, due
Ilfracombe 2.15 p.m. Leave Ilfracombe 5.15 p.m., due Penarth 9.15 p.m.
10.15 a.m. Combined Steamer and Coach Tour via WESTON to CHEDDAR
GORGE. Leave Weston 8.30 p.m. for Penarth. Coach leaves Knightstone
Garage (opposite Marine Lake) 2.00 p.m.

SUNDAY, APRIL 22nd
12.40 p.m. Afternoon Trip to PORTISHEAD and BRISTOL, due to arrive
Portishead 1.55 p.m., Bristol 2.50 p.m. Leave Bristol 5.15 p.m. Portishead
6 p.m. for Penarth, due 7.35 p.m.
12.40 p.m. Long Cruise calling at Bristol thence down the River Avon towards
Clevedon, afterwards again calling at Bristol before returning to Penarth,
arriving about 7.35 p.m.

TUESDAY, MAY 1st
9.00 a.m. Day Trip to ILFRACOMBE and LUNDY ISLAND (to land). Due
Ilfracombe 12.10 p.m., Lundy Island 2.00 p.m. Leave Lundy Island 4.50 p.m.,
Ilfracombe 6.45 p.m. for Penarth, due 9.35 p.m.

SATURDAY, MAY 5th
10.15 a.m. Long Day Trip to ILFRACOMBE and LUNDY ISLAND (to land).
Due Ilfracombe 2.00 p.m., Lundy Island 3.50 p.m. Leave Lundy Island 5.50
p.m., Ilfracombe 7.35 p.m. direct for Penarth, due 10.45 p.m.

SUNDAY, MAY 6th
11.35 a.m. Afternoon Trip to PORTISHEAD and BRISTOL, due to arrive
Portishead 12.50 p.m., Bristol 1.50 p.m. Leave Bristol 4.00 p.m., Portishead
4.45 p.m. for Penarth, due 6.20 p.m.
11.35 a.m. Long Cruise calling at Bristol thence down the River Avon towards
Clevedon, afterwards again calling at Bristol before returning to Penarth,
arriving about 6.20 p.m.

BANK HOLIDAY MONDAY, MAY 7th
WESTON. Leave Penarth 12.50 p.m. Leave Weston 6.45 p.m.
5.45 p.m. Cruise across the Channel, back 7.35 p.m.

THURSDAY, MAY 10th
8.45 a.m. Long Day Trip to ILFRACOMBE and LUNDY ISLAND (to land).
The steamer sails direct to Ilfracombe due 11.35 a.m. and Lundy island due
1.25 p.m. Leave Lundy island 4.00 p.m., Ilfracombe 5.45 p.m. direct for Penarth
due 9.35 p.m.

For further sailings, fares and conditions see overleaf

Handbill for early season sailings from Penarth from 16 April to 20 May 1979.

Arriving at Ilfracombe on 13 July 1969, this photograph clearly shows that there was no cowl on the funnel at this time.

In a rather rusty end-of-season condition, going astern out of Ilfracombe, returning to Weston, Penarth and Cardiff, on 27 September 1969.

Departing from Ilfracombe on 15 June 1969, her first day in service on the Bristol Channel.

Anchored at Lundy, seen from PS *Waverley* on their first meeting, 3 June 1979.

Departing from Ilfracombe in 1980.

Enthusiast Phil Tolley looks out at the coast on a non-landing cruise from Ilfracombe on Easter Day, 30 March 1975.

Balmoral at Ilfracombe in June 1980.

Arriving at Ilfracombe in 1979. The photograph was taken from the old car deck, now enclosed and the location of the dining saloon.

The car deck from the promenade deck, 1978, showing the area now utilised by the dining salon and galley.

Balmoral lying at Lundy on 21 June 1969, on one of her first ever visits to the island.

Above: Anchored off Lundy, seen from the tender, taking passengers ashore, August 1970.

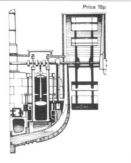

Price 15p

P. & A. CAMPBELL LTD.
In 1854 the keel of Brunel's Great Eastern was laid at Millwall on the Thames. In this same year whilst Brunel's great five funnelled paddle leviathan was taking shape, we first started operating paddle excursion steamers on the Clyde. Brunel's wonder ship has passed on long ago, but we have gone on operating excursion steamers, out of Bristol since 1887 and two World Wars apart, ever since. An early steamer, the MAIL, became a blockade runner in the American Civil War. The paddle steamer CAMBRIA, built in 1896, and broken up shortly after the 1939-45 War is reputed to have been the fastest passenger steamer of her size afloat, whilst the famous BRITANNIA, withdrawn in 1956, after almost sixty year's service was beloved by generations of Bristolians as "our ship". We carried Victoria's tightly corseted and whiskered subjects, laden with bottled stout and pork pies to Victoria's Golden Jubilee Fleet Review in 1887. We were at the Diamond Jubilee Review in 1897. In fact, at every major Fleet Review ever since, culminating in the Queen's Silver Jubilee Review at Spithead in 1977. Today our motorships BALMORAL and DEVONIA carry on the Campbell tradition and we hope you will have a happy and pleasant voyage.

m.v. BALMORAL
Gower Restaurant

Souvenir Menu 1980

HOT MEALS

Egg, Bacon, Sausage, Bread, Beans	95p
Grill and Chips	£2.15p
Sausage and Chips	60p
Gammon and Chips	£1.78p
Chicken and Chips	£1.83p
Pie and Chips	£1.30p
Plaice and Chips	£1.50p
Cod and Chips	£1.40p
Beef or Chicken, and Vegetables	£1.80p
Sirloin Steak	£3.70p
Cottage Pie and Chips or Boiled Potatoes	£1.60p
Scampi and Chips	£2.40p

SNACKS

Sandwiches	45p
Pasties	40p
Sausage Rolls	30p
Beefburgers	45p
Soup	30p
Cereal	35p
Biscuits (3)	10p
Bread and Butter	15p

SWEETS

Apple Pie	40p
Cheese Cake	60p
Fruit Cocktail	35p
Fruit and Jelly	35p

DRINKS

Tea	16p
Coffee	25p
Coke 9 oz.	33p
Fruit Juice	25p
Shandy	33p
Lemonade	30p
Orange Drink	15p
Chocolate	25p
Beef Drink	20p
Choice of Cold Buffet when available	£2.50p

A restaurant menu for the 1980 season.

The Brave Attempt: MV *Prince Ivanhoe* leaving Largs in June 1981, prior to her Bristol Channel season in that year.

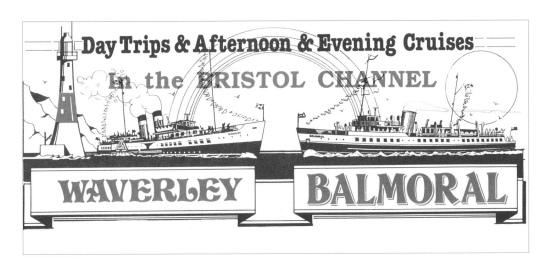

An advertising poster for *Balmoral* and her fleet-mate *Waverley* in the Bristol Channel area.

A decal showing '*Balmoral* Classic Cruise Ship' in her post-1995 colour scheme.

Balmoral in her 1987-1991 livery at Cumberland Basin, Bristol, with Brunel's Clifton Suspension Bridge in the background. The pontoon at Hotwells Landing Stage had been removed after the 1971 season.

Arriving at Bristol on 16 October 1995, on a special sailing for the centenary celebration of Penarth Pier and the specially painted funnel, taken from PS *Waverley*.

Arriving at Cumberland basin, Bristol, during her celebration maiden voyage weekend. Note the early colour scheme under WSN ownership, with the very light-green boot topping.

Balmoral lying on the grid-iron at Cumberland basin, Bristol, at low tide, September 1996, one of the last occasions when this was used. The grid-iron is now completely submerged beneath the mud.

Balmoral in David Abel's dry dock
at Bristol in her early years in preservation.

In winter lay up at Bristol in her 1987-1991 colour scheme, covered in snow, with the WSN launch
Westward Ho alongside.

At Prince's Landing Stage, Bristol, from the Lundy packet *Oldenburg*.

Proceeding up the River Avon.

Arriving at Clevedon Pier on a trial berthing prior to the official reopening in 1988.

Passengers at Steep Holm beach embarking on the tender *Silver Spray*, July 1992. *Balmoral* is prowling up and down. Captain Kit Lee was anxious about the increasing swell and the potential difficulties for the passenger transfer back to his ship.

Balmoral at Watchet on 7 August 1996, operating a trip from Penarth to Watchet and Minehead with a cruise to off Porlock

Balmoral at Minehead in her 1994 condition.

Berthed at Ilfracombe on 27 April 1986, on one of her very early WSN calls.

At the Stone Bench, Ilfracombe, on 22 August 1987.

Balmoral at Ilfracombe at 0550 on 11 August 1999, getting ready to take a capacity crowd to view the total eclipse of the sun off Trevose Head.

Departing the new Stone Bench at Ilfracombe on 8 August 2006.

Tendering at Lundy went on until the pier was built in 2000.

Miss Barbara Brown enjoys a great day at Lundy in 1987. *Balmoral's* white colour scheme of the early preservation years was intended to make resemble a motor yacht. Miss Brown was a great supporter of *Balmoral*.

At the new pier on Lundy, *Oldenburg* seen from *Balmoral*, August 2003.

In P&A Campbell days, the Lundy tenders were named after their paddle steamers of the past, like *Lady Moyra*, seen here in 1979. She commemorated the paddle steamer built in 1903 as *Gwalia* for the Barry Railway, which was sold in 1910 to the Furness Railway, and came under P&A Campbell ownership in 1922. She was renamed *Brighton Queen* in 1933, being lost at Dunkirk in 1940.

In July 1996, at Bideford on the River Torridge.

Balmoral on one of her occasional trips to the Cornish port of Padstow between 1987 and 1991.

Captain Steve Michel manoeuvres *Balmoral* alongside at Padstow. Captain Michel has served on Balmoral from 1986 to the present.

In dry dock at Sharpness in April 1997, following bow repairs.

Balmoral moored at the lock entrance, Lydney, on 11 September 1997, on one of her occasional calls there.

Balmoral at Newport (Gwent) in July 1992. She was arriving to cruise to Clevedon and Steep Holm (to land). A party of the Newport Harbour Commissioners travelled on board on this occasion on their annual day out to Weston.

Balmoral arriving at Penarth on 15 October 2000, deputising for *Waverley*, which had been delayed getting from the Thames by bad weather. *Balmoral* was about to transfer passengers and stores to her senior sister.

Balmoral off Penarth in her current livery.

Balmoral off Penarth while *Waverley* lies at the pier on 26 May 2004. Such meetings of the company's two ships are very rare.

At Barry Island old harbour on 29 August 1998 whilst on a trip from Penarth to Ilfracombe.

Balmoral at Porthcawl on 10 August 1999, bringing in returning afternoon cruise passengers before departing on a single journey to Ilfracombe.

Balmoral at Tenby on 17 September 2001. This call had been rescheduled from Milford Haven due to unfavourable tide conditions at the latter port. *Balmoral* was about to depart on a single light journey to Glasgow to take up her traditional September holiday weekend sailings.

Arriving at the low tide berth of one of the Bristol Channel piers on 26 June 1992. Do you know where this is? If so, please contact the authors.

Chapter 3: Liverpool & North Wales

This area for many is the highlight of any *Balmoral* timetable. Round Anglesey is a first-class trip, sailing though the notorious Menai Straits under the bridges is a superb experience. Sadly, the area lost out with the closure of its holiday pier at Llandudno in 2006, although WEL have braved it out, providing coach transfers to *Balmoral* at Menai Bridge.

Back in her P&A Campbell days, *Balmoral* appeared in the area for very short spells. Since 1986 she has made it her own for an all-too-brief ten-day period each year

On 14 May 1971 *Balmoral* made a charter sailing for the Coastal Cruising Association from Liverpool to Llandudno and the Menai Straits, followed by a cruise round Puffin Island. She is seen here at Liverpool Landing Stage with the Isle of Man Steam Packet Co.'s pioneer car ferry *Manx Maid* ahead of her.

At Liverpool Landing Stage on the same occasion.

A stern view at the landing stage on the same day.

Balmoral leaving Llandudno later the same day.

Above: CCA Council member John Bird checks tickets as passengers embark at Llandudno.

Left: Departing Llandudno with the Little Orme in the background.

Balmoral at St George's Pier, Menai Bridge, on the same cruise.

Berthed facing the other way at Menai Bridge.

Telford's suspension bridge seen looking aft from *Balmoral*, berthed at St George's Pier, Menai Bridge.

The final destination of the CCA charter on 14 May 1971 – Puffin Island.

Balmoral at Liverpool Landing Stage, at the Mersey Ferries pontoon.

Balmoral leaving Seacombe on 29 May 1993 for a return sailing to Llandudno. This was a special sailing for the Battle of the Atlantic celebrations and had attracted a capacity crowd. Many passengers were booked to return by coach.

Above: Stormbound at Seacombe on 20 June 2003. *Balmoral* had departed Liverpool at 10.45 for Llandudno with 520 passengers aboard, but had had to abort the trip due to bad weather.

Left: A 2008 handbill for trips from Menai Bridge, Caernarfon and Liverpool.

Balmoral berthed at Ellesmere Port on 1 June 2002 on a cruise from Llandudno and Liverpool.

At Ellesmere Port on 15 September 1991 on a cruise from Menai Bridge, Llandudno and Liverpool.

Balmoral at Mostyn on 28 May 2002, on a trip from Menai Bridge and Llandudno.

Balmoral at the North Wales pier of Llandudno. This pier has been closed since 2006 because of the poor condition of the landing stage, and the lack of money to get it repaired. Passengers are now taken from here by coach, normally to Menai Bridge, to join the vessel.

Departing from Llandudno - one of the most spectacular Victorian piers in the UK.

Menai Bridge, St George's Pier on 6 June 2005. *Balmoral* had recently arrived from Liverpool on a sailing diverted from Llandudno due to strong north-easterly winds.

A deck view approaching the Britannia Bridge in the Menai Straits.

In the Menai Straits in 2003; this photograph shows the Britannia railway bridge and Telford's suspension bridge in the background.

Another healthy load circumnavigating *Ynys Mon* (Anglesey) in May 1997, seen here at Caernarfon.

Balmoral on one of her infrequent visits to Blackpool North Pier. Note that her anchor has been lowered.

Balmoral approaching Morecambe on a sailing from Menai Bridge, Llandudno and Blackpool. Passengers were waiting to board for an afternoon cruise on Morecambe bay.

Balmoral at Barrow Ramsden dock entrance on 10 May 1994. Possibly she may have been diverted from either Morecambe or Blackpool because of the prevailing weather.

Chapter 4: The Irish Sea & Isle of Man

Balmoral has operated in the waters around north and north-east Ireland, the Isle of Man and north-west England extending to Wigtownshire in Scotland during late May and early June each year. Cruises have lasted for one to three days only in recent seasons. In particular, sailings from the Great Britain to Manx waters prove very popular and are often fully loaded. The Manx coast seen from *Balmoral* makes a beautiful cruise, an otherwise hidden journey. Her cruises round the Antrim and County Down coast and into Strangford Lough have become very limited now, but still provide the passenger with fantastic days out. Not until the *Waverley* years were such trips available to many of the places served.

In May 1970, *Balmoral* visited Douglas in order to tender to the Swedish America Lines' *Kungsholm*. She is seen here, berthed at Victoria Pier, Douglas, on 16 May that year.

Departing Douglas, with a ton-class minesweeper moored at Battery Pier,

At that time the Isles of Scilly Steamship Co.'s *Queen of the Isles* (1964) was operating on charter to Norwest Hovercraft on the Fleetwood to Douglas service, pending the arrival from overhaul of MacBrayne's *Lochiel*, which was to become their *Norwest Laird*. She is seen here from *Balmoral* at Douglas on 17 May 1970. She only operated on the route for three days, from 16 to 18 May.

Berthed at Whitehaven, shortly to depart for a trip to the Isle of Man.

Balmoral at her overnight berth in the inner docks at Whitehaven on 12 June 2004. Loading started for her day trip to Douglas, Isle of Man, shortly after this photo was taken.

Arriving at Workington on 31 May 1999 for a sailing to Ramsey, Douglas and a Manx coast cruise. *Balmoral's* arrival here was delayed awaiting a sufficient depth of water.

Above: At Garlieston on the
Wigtownshire coast, from where she
normally makes two day-return trips
to the Isle of Man on consecutive days
around early June each year.

Right: A handbill for the sailing from
Garlieston to the Isle of Man on 17 June
1990, the first season in which this was
offered.

SAIL AWAY ON THE CLASSIC SHIP BALMORAL

The M. V. Balmoral has been restored in association with
The Paddle Steamer Preservation Society and the famous WAVERLEY.
On board you will enjoy the heated lounges - restaurant - bar - souvenir shop
and you must bring the children for an adventure they will always remember.
BALMORAL cruises at 14 knots and can carry 700 passengers.

DON'T MISS THE GRAND DAY TRIP TO THE ISLE OF MAN

SATURDAY JUNE 17 LEAVE GARLIESTON (Wigtown) 10 am   ARRIVE BACK 9.45 pm
Sail to the Isle of Man, passing Point of Ayre and Ramsey to
Douglas for 5 hours ashore £15.95. Children under 16 £7.95 OR
stay aboard and cruise right round the Island £10.95. Children
under 16 £9.95.
TO BE SURE OF YOUR TICKETS
· book by Access or Visa · Telephone: 041 221 8152 or book in advance at
A. T. Mays, The Travel Agents, 216 King Street, Castle Douglas · Telephone: 2811,
4/6 Great King St., Dumfries · Telephone 63968, 20 Bridge St., Stranraer · Telephone: 3611,
· R. Houston, Harbour Master, 13 North Crescent, Garlieston · Telephone 259
OR BUY YOUR TICKETS ON BOARD WHEN YOU SAIL.

P.S. WAVERLEY Summer Sailings commence on the Clyde on June 20
a full timetable is available on board or on request from Waverley Office.

IN ASSOCIATION WITH
WAVERLEY EXCURSIONS LTD. THE PADDLE STEAMER PRESERVATION SOCIETY
A REGISTERED CHARITY
WAVERLEY TERMINAL · ANDERSTON QUAY, GLASGOW · TELEPHONE: 041 221 8152

All tickets are issued and all passengers and others are carried subject to the terms and conditions of Waverley Excursions Ltd., a
copy of which is available on request from the Company's Offices or on demand from the Purser at the gangway before going on
board the Steamer. All sailings are subject to weather, visibility and circumstances permitting. Catering offered subject to availability.

WAVERLEY EXCURSIONS LTD., WAVERLEY TERMINAL, GLASGOW · TELEPHONE: 041 221 8152

RESTAURANT ★ BAR ★ HEATED LOUNGES

Above: *Balmoral* arriving at Garlieston in her 1987-1991 livery.

Left: Berthed at Edward Pier, Douglas, in the same livery.

Having arrived at Douglas from Whitehaven on 31 May 2003, *Balmoral* is departing for an afternoon cruise to the Calf of Man and Port St Mary.

Entering Ramsey harbour entrance in her 1987-1991 colour scheme.

At Port Erin, Raglan Pier, on Tynwald Day, 6 July 1992. *Balmoral* is on a round-the-island cruise, calling at Douglas, Peel, Port Erin and Port St Mary.

A handbill for 1988 sailings from Belfast and Carrickfergus, the highlights of which were sailings to Donaghadee, Portaferry and Killyleagh on Saturday 4 June, and to Larne and Red Bay on Sunday 5 June and Saturday 11 June.

Right: *Balmoral* berthed at Pollock Dock, Belfast, in 1990.

Below: Arriving at Bangor, Co. Down.

Balmoral at Portaferry, at the entrance to Strangford Lough, on 19 June 1990.

Arriving at Portaferry in 1988.

At the working port of Warrenpoint, in the 1987-1991 colours with the 'go-faster stripes' on the bow.

At the pier on the island of Rathlin. Trips have been offered to here twice from Ayr and Campbeltown, and more frequently from Northern Irish ports.

Balmoral at Rathlin from sea level.

Berthed at Ballycastle Old Pier.

Balmoral at Ballycastle ferry terminal, showing her forward saloon windows weather-boarded for a light sailing round Scotland to the Firth of Forth.

Turning in the River Bann at Coleraine in 1993, with passengers on the quayside anxious to get aboard her.

Balmoral on the River Foyle at Londonderry.

At Bantry in the southwest of Ireland on a one-off visit for a tall ships event.

At Castletownbere on the same occasion, being tendered to by the car ferry *Misneach*, a sister of CalMac's island-class car ferries.

Chapter 5: The Firth of Clyde

These are home waters for that wonderful old paddle steamer, *Waverley*, which appears off season on the Bristol Channel, as her fleet-mate *Balmoral*, in her off season, appears on the Clyde. Since 1986 *Balmoral* has become an honorary Clyde steamer, as from time to time she has called at places *Waverley* cannot, including Ormidale, Carrick Castle, Sandbank, Lamlash and the new pier facility at the 1A berth at Gourock.

During her brief four-day spell in the autumn she keeps alive the Millport Illuminations & Fireworks cruise, now a long-established end to the cruising season. It also brings *Balmoral* into an area of rich maritime history, with the origins of Campbell's at Kilmun, before the move to the Bristol Channel in 1887. *Balmoral* was their last vessel in 1979-80. Also, J I Thornycroft & Co., *Balmoral's* builders, are now part of the BVT Surface Ships consortium operating the former Yarrow naval shipyard at Scotstoun.

Balmoral passing Ailsa Craig on a light run to the Clyde in September 1989.

Balmoral seen from *Waverley* at Anderston Quay in 1985, shortly after she had arrived from Dundee, but prior to any work being done on her.

Seen from across the river at Anderston Quay in September 1985.

Approaching Renfrew during the September weekend in 1988.

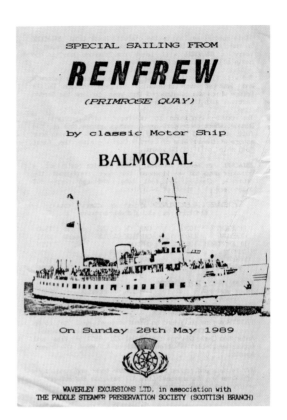

SPECIAL SAILING FROM

RENFREW

(PRIMROSE QUAY)

by classic Motor Ship

BALMORAL

On Sunday 28th May 1989

WAVERLEY EXCURSIONS LTD. in association with
THE PADDLE STEAMER PRESERVATION SOCIETY (SCOTTISH BRANCH)

Seemingly home-made handbill for a sailing on 28 May 1989 from Renfrew (Primrose Quay) upriver to Glasgow, then to Helensburgh, Dunoon and Carrick Castle.

Balmoral gave some sailings from the Pudzeoch (referred to in the previous item as Primrose Quay) at Renfrew in that era, where she is seen here. Such a call would be impossible nowadays because of redevelopment of the area and the building of houses and flats there.

At the entrance to Rothesay Dock in Clydebank on 28 September 2008. In earlier years berths inside Rothesay Dock have been used for calls at Clydebank.

Sailing upriver passing Dumbarton rock.

Unusually berthed at Gourock, the HQ of ferry operator Caledonian MacBrayne, at the 1A berth on 2 October 2008.

Balmoral berthed at Kilcreggan on 22 September 1990.

Balmoral, dressed overall for the *QE2* farewell sailings, with CalMac's *Jupiter* and a Western Ferries vessel at Hunter's quay in the background, 5 October 2008.

Berthed at Kilmun on her only call there: back to her Campbell roots.

At the rarely used pier of Sandbank in the Holy Loch on 25 September 2002

Balmoral on the occasion of her first call at Carrick Castle on 22 May 1989.

A later call at Carrick Castle, showing the renovation work under way on the Castle to re-roof it and make it habitable again.

Another view of Carrick Castle, this time in 2001, with a small portion of the red funnel just visible to the left of the wheelhouse and the brown wood-effect bridge front, painted so for the BBC charter for *Crowdie and Cream*.

Balmoral at Rothesay on 26 September 1997, at the berth now exclusively used by CalMac.

Passing through the narrows in the Kyles of Bute with the late George C. Train on board. George Train founded the Coastal Cruising Association in 1964.

High tide at Tighnabruaich in her present condition.

Tighnabruaich in 1992, her green-hulled year, with a yellow funnel

Approaching Largs on 14 May 1994, with her green-topped yellow funnel and flying the Clyde River Steamer Club pennant, en route to her unique call at Lamlash.

Balmoral leaving Largs in 2002 and turning to head north for Dunoon.

Balmoral at Millport in 1993 with her red funnel.

Balmoral and *Waverley* meeting at Millport in 1999, their only meeting on the Firth of Clyde to date.

Departing Brodick in her 1987-1991 colours.

In the shadow of Goat Fell, seen from *Caledonian Isles*, on 16 July 2000. During this period she deputised for *Waverley*, which was completing her rebuild. She was sailing south after a charter, having sailed light from the Thames to Glasgow. She then did one day's charter for a wedding, then headed south to Bristol to pick up her schedule.

Berthed at Campbeltown in June 1993, en route from Ayr to Rathlin.

At Campbeltown with *Claymore*, at that time operating the ferry service to Ballycastle for the Argyll & Antrim Steam Packet Co. Ltd, which operated between 1997 and 1999.

A bow view of 20 September 2007, arriving at Greenock Custom House Quay on a sailing to escort *Queen Elizabeth 2* on departure from her river of birth after her penultimate visit.

A packed *Balmoral* on the same occasion. This shows the French grey colour of the upper hull, the traditional P&A Campbell colour.

Left: Seen from ahead, the same day.

Below: And from the stern quarter off Dunoon.

Heeling as she takes a sharp turn to starboard as she is followed by *QE2* departing the Firth.

On a beautiful day on the Firth of Clyde.

Chapter 6: The West Highlands

Balmoral has made only a handful of visits to the West Highlands, the majority of these replacing *Waverley* which has not been available for various reasons. On about five occasions now, *Balmoral* has cruised the waters made famous by MacBrayne's fabled *King George V*. She has visited Canna, Gigha and Port Askaig, all piers that *Waverley* is unable to call at owing to a short berth or awkward approaches. *Balmoral* has cruised close to the shore of much of this area during light sailings.

Balmoral at Kennacraig with the Islay Ferry *Isle of Arran* in 1999.

At Gigha Pier on 30 April 1994 on a cruise from Fort William and Oban.

At Port Askaig, Islay, with the hills of Jura behind.

RMS *Balmoral* at Colonsay on 30 April 1994, when she made an unscheduled call en route from Oban to Gigha to land the mails.

Arriving at Oban, with Kerrera and the mountains of Mull in the background, in the briefly applied 1994 livery.

Berthed at Oban North Pier. Note the old pier buildings, replaced by two modern glass-enclosed restaurants in recent years.

At Oban Railway Pier, in the space now occupied by the Number 2 link span.

Balmoral at Fort William in 1994.

On a unique call at Canna in the Small Isles in 2000, deputising for *Waverley* during the latter's rebuild.

Chapter 7: North & East Scotland

This is a very treacherous coast for any shipping company. WSN Co. is the only pleasure steamer operator ever to have offered a series of cruises from the northern part of this area. *Waverley* has only sailed to Aberdeen to refuel, and then only three times. *Balmoral* has, as you will see from the list of piers called at, been everywhere from Scrabster to Berwick-upon-Tweed at some time or other. She has revived the Forth pleasure sailings of the pre-1914 Galloway Saloon Steam Packet Co.

It has certainly made for some memorable trips, and the delight of seeing the Forth and Tay bridges, Isle of May, Bass Rock and Stroma from the coastal steamer's deck. However, the finest sailings on this part of the coast were up the Tay to Perth and round Lindisfarne and the Farne Islands, all absolutely outstanding trips.

Balmoral and the Stromness ferry *St Ola* (III), of P&O, then in her second year in service for the company, at Scrabster in July 1993.

Arriving at Inverness, having just passed under the Kessock Bridge, 21 May 1988.

Balmoral moored at Stonehaven, June 1995, having just returned from a cruise to Montrose and round the Bass Rock.

At Montrose, very much a commercial port on the River South Esk, on the same day.

Balmoral in her pre-preservation guise, at Dundee on 16 February 1985, as a disused floating pub.

At Dundee in her 1993, green-hulled condition, with passengers waiting to board.

In the River Tay near Perth, in her current condition.

Balmoral at Leith for the tall ships gathering on 15 July 1995.

Balmoral at Granton in 1988.

Approaching the Forth Road Bridge and Rail Bridge from upstream.

SAIL AWAY ON THE CLASS

Restored in association with the Paddle Stea
On board you will enjoy the heate
and you must bring the children fc
BALMORAL cruises at 14 I

FOR A FEV

FROM ST. ANDREWS

SATURDAY MAY 13 LEAVE ST. ANDREWS 10 am   ARRIVE BACK 9.30 pm
Sail round Fife Ness to Anstruther £5.95, Children under 16 £2.95
then past Inchkeith to Granton £9.95, Children under 16 £4.95 or
Grand Full Day Cruise in the Firth of Forth and 'Under the Bridges'
£14.95, Children under 16 £7.50
BE SURE OF YOUR TICKETS - book in advance at A. T. Mays - The
Travel Agents 37 Bell Street, St. Andrews - Telephone: 74451 or 22
Bonnygate, Cupar - Telephone: 52556.
OR BUY YOUR TICKETS ON BOARD WHEN YOU SAIL.

FROM ANSTRUTHER

SATURDAY MAY 13 LEAVE ANSTRUTHER 11.15 am   ARRIVE BACK 8.15 pm
Sail across the Firth past Inchkeith to Granton £7.95, Children under
16 £3.95 or stay aboard to cruise 'Under the Bridges' £12.95,
Children under 16 £6.50.

SUNDAY MAY 21 LEAVE ANSTRUTHER 2 pm   ARRIVE BACK 4.30 pm
Cruise round the Isle of May £5.95, Children under 16 £2.95.
BE SURE OF YOUR TICKETS - book in advance at Scottish Fisheries
Museum - Telephone: 310628.
OR BUY YOUR TICKETS ON BOARD WHEN YOU SAIL.

Restaurant ★ Bar ★ Heated Lounges

A handbill for the sailings on the Firth of Forth from the Fife ports of St Andrews, Anstruther, Burntisland and Aberdour from 13 to 22 May 1989. Note the 'Balmoral: the Classic Cruise ship' logo that was in use at that time.

PASSENGER SHIP BALMORAL

eservation Society and the famous WAVERLEY.
ies - restaurant - bar - souvenir shop
dventure they will always remember.
nd can carry 700 passengers

YS ONLY

FROM BURNTISLAND — Ferry Slip

SUNDAY MAY 14   LEAVE BURNTISLAND 12.30 pm   ARRIVE BACK 8 pm* by coach
Sail across to Granton £4.95, Children under 16 £2.50 or stay aboard
for a Grand Cruise round the Islands of the Firth - Inchkeith - Fidra -
Craigleith - Bass Rock and towards Dunbar. £11.95
Children under 16 £5.95.

THURSDAY MAY 18   LEAVE BURNTISLAND 11.30 am   ARRIVE BACK 3.30 pm
Sail across to the Lothian coast and cruise round the Bass Rock £7.95.
SENIOR CITIZENS £4.95.

SATURDAY MAY 20   LEAVE BURNTISLAND 12.45 pm   ARRIVE BACK 7.30* by coach
Sail up river 'Under the Bridges' to Bo'ness £11.95, Children under
16 £5.95. (Book on board for a trip on the steam railway).

MONDAY MAY 22   LEAVE BURNTISLAND 1.45 pm   ARRIVE BACK 6.30 pm
Sail to Aberdour and then cruise 'Under the Bridges' round Inchkeith
- Inchcolm and its Abbey £9.95, Children under 16 £4.95.
BE SURE OF YOUR TICKETS - book in advance at J.S. McCracken
265 High Street, Burntisland - Telephone: 872292 or A.T. Mays - Travel
Agents 64 High Street, Kirkcaldy - Telephone: 261365 or Maygate,
Dunfermline - Telephone: 722841.
OR BUY YOUR TICKETS ON BOARD WHEN YOU SAIL.

FROM ABERDOUR — Stone Pier

MONDAY MAY 22   LEAVE ABERDOUR 3 pm   ARRIVE BACK 5.30 pm
Afternoon cruise 'Under the Bridges' - round Inchkeith - Inchcolm and
its Abbey £7.95, Children under 16 £3.95.
BUY YOUR TICKETS ON BOARD WHEN YOU SAIL.

Book by Access or Visa
Telephone: 041-221 8152

A Timetable of the complete sailings for Waverley and Balmoral around Britain,
can be obtained on board or from Waverley Terminal, Glasgow.

WAVERLEY EXCURSIONS LTD. IN ASSOCIATION WITH THE PADDLE STEAMER PRESERVATION SOCIETY
A REGISTERED CHARITY

WAVERLEY TERMINAL - ANDERSTON QUAY, GLASGOW — TELEPHONE 041-221 8152

The reverse of this offered sailings from Grangemouth, Bo'ness and Granton.

Balmoral passes under the Forth Rail Bridge, over the house tops of Sorth Queensferry.

At Bo'ness on a unique call to connect with the Bo'ness and Kinneil steam railway in 1989.

The seabird colony of the Bass Rock, off North Berwick, a very popular cruise destination on the Firth of Forth.

Moored on the outer sea wall at Anstruther, a fishing village in the East Neuk of Fife, and the only such village having a harbour large and deep enough to berth *Balmoral*.

Chapter 8: The East Coast of England

Again this is a wild coastline, but very pleasurable in parts. *Balmoral* has offered many chances to sail from the Tyne and Tees, up into the heart of Whitby, into the lovely harbour at Scarborough and up the Humber to Goole and Keadby. These have not been so well supported, but at least those who sailed on these unique cruises will have good tales to tell of unparalleled coastal voyages

Balmoral departing from Amble. Amble is the only harbour on the Northumberland Coast north of Blyth able to take a ship the size of *Balmoral*. She has normally sailed from here on non-landing trips to the Farne Islands, on a single trip to Leith, southwards to Hartlepool or up the Tyne to Newcastle.

Arriving at Whitby on 18 July 1993 on an east coast cruise.

At Scarborough on 10 June 1994, on a cruise from Middlesbrough and Hartlepool. The green hull used in that season is seen to advantage in this shot.

Arriving at Hull riverside quay on 18 June 1994 for a cruise to Goole. A familiar face prepares to take the ropes.

Right: Balmoral at Grimsby en route from Hull to Keadby on 19 June 1994.

Below: At Keadby, on the River Trent, with a good crowd having arrived from Hull and Grimsby on 19 June 1994.

Chapter 9: The Thames & Medway

This is an area vital to the company, sailings including many sell-out single trips by both *Balmoral* and *Waverley*, returning by coach, with an opportunity to view Tower Bridge open or to view the Thames landmarks floodlit. It also allows links to the Medway to view the river paddle steamer *Kingswear Castle* of 1924, also fully preserved in association with the PSPS.

  The Thames is not the most attractive of rivers in its lower reaches, but at least the *Balmoral* brings alive the thoughts of many favourite outings to Southend or Whitstable, Clacton or the River Medway, made by millions on the Thames steamers of yesteryear.

Open up them pearly gates! Passing through Tower Bridge on June 1995, one of the 'must do' experiences of *Balmoral's* sailings.

Approaching Tower Bridge from Tower Pier in her 1987-1991 livery. Note the shadow of the bridge.

Just going through Tower Bridge to shortly arrive at Tower Pier with a full load of passengers from Whitstable and intermediate piers, 1 May 1993.

Balmoral at London Bridge City Pier with a Thames sailing barge on 25 June 1995. She had just arrived from Colchester and intermediate piers.

Off Tilbury with Polish Ocean Lines' transatlantic liner *Stefan Batory* on 26 September 1987.

At Whitstable, berthed ahead of PS *Kingswear Castle*, on 26 September 1987. Captain John Megoran surveys the scene.

Cruises from :Chatham :: LONDON

September 24 until Oct

BALMORAL ⊚ WAVERLEY ⊚ ⊚

THE SHIPS OF THE PADDLE STEAMER PRESERVATION SOCIETY FLEET

from GRAVESEND & TILBURY LANDING STAGE

PASSENGERS FROM GRAVESEND JOIN THE FERRY FOR TILBURY.
THERE IS NO EXTRA CHARGE FOR THE FERRY CROSSING TO JOIN WAVERLEY'S CRUISES FROM TILBURY

TILBURY : GRAVESEND : SOUTHEND

er 4 ·· 1987

INGSWEAR CASTLE
INTAGE RIVER PADDLE STEAMER

ruises from Chatham – Sun Pier & Strood

KINGSWEAR CASTLE Now Sails from CHATHAM-SUN PIER (5 minutes from The Pentagon) & Strood
Pier 2 minutes walk from Strood Railway Station.

Above: handbill for trips from Gravesend, Tilbury, Chatham and Strood for the period form 24 September to 4 October 1987, with a header showing *Waverley*, *Balmoral*, and *Kingswear Castle* as well as a Thames barge. This was the year *Balmoral* covered for *Waverley*, which was out of service with boiler trouble.

Left: Berthed in Ramsgate harbour on 21 June 1992.

Arriving at Colchester for a cruise to Winvenhoe, Clacton and London Bridge City Pier on 25 June 1995.

Balmoral arriving at Walton-on-the-Naze on 3 July 1994 en route to Great Yarmouth.

Chapter 10: Special sailings

This section touches on those unique trips, never to be repeated, some as far and wide as to the French and Dutch coasts.

These include Brighton in 1968, Ormidale on Loch Riddon in 1990, Calais and Rotterdam in 2006, and Lamlash in Arran, where *Balmoral* was the first large passenger vessel to berth since 1955. Boulogne was a non-passport sailing, common back in the early 1950s on *Glen Gower*, one of *Balmoral's* contemporaries in the coastal steamer scene of that era.

Balmoral has been a valuable covering for *Waverley* in periods of difficulty:

1987	She covered the autumn Solent and Thames schedules. *Waverley* was withdrawn due to major boiler trouble (MV *Southsea* covered in the Firth of Clyde)
1991	Covered Solent and Thames (late autumn) when *Waverley* was off with port paddle-wheel failure.
2000*	Covered for *Waverley* when she was having phase one rebuild (until August)
2003*	Covered for *Waverley's* phase two rebuild, both these at Great Yarmouth (until June)
2008*	Covered for *Waverley* (in part) which was withdrawn until July with port paddle-shaft and keyway trouble.

During all of these periods of both foreseen and unforeseen problems, the value of *Balmoral* cannot be overemphasised. Her contribution to WSN/WEL has from time to time been put in the spotlight. The above list stands to prove her worth where the alternative was no revenue being generated, in most cases for long periods.
* During these periods valuable parts of *Balmoral's* schedule were worked into the relief sailings for *Waverley*.

Left: Off Brighton Palace Pier on 16 June 1968, on a special Coastal Cruising Association charter from Southampton, Southsea, Littlehampton, where passengers were embarked and disembarked by tender, and Worthing. Although near the pier, she did not call on that occasion.

Below: *Balmoral* at Penzance with the Isles of Scilly Steamship Co.'s *Scillonian III* on 21 June 1992. In May 1991 she deputised for the latter on the Isles of Scilly mail service for a spell when *Scillonian III* was suffering from engine trouble, and again on 19-20 June of the following year to enable the mail vessel to undertake a special sailing to Guernsey.

At Ormidale in Loch Riddon on the occasion of a special sailing on 26 May 1990.

At Ormidale on the same occasion, showing the grassy pier there.

Arriving at Lamlash, returning from a special round Holy Isle cruise on 14 May 1994 on a charter for the Clyde River Steamer Club.

Berthed at Lamlash, on the unique visit there on 14 May 1994.

CLYDE RIVER STEAMER CLUB
SATURDAY 14 MAY 1994
SPECIAL CRUISE
by m.v. BALMORAL
via the Kyles of Bute
to BRODICK, LAMLASH
and ROUND HOLY ISLE

0053   0053

The Edmondson card ticket issued for this unique cruise.

Balmoral has made very occasional sailings to continental ports, and is seen here at Calais in 2006 for a tall ships race.

Tall ships at Calais from the foredeck of *Balmoral*.

Balmoral at Boulogne in June 1996.

These sailings bring to mind the excursions undertaken by P&A Campbell paddle steamers from Sussex coast piers to Boulogne. These were operated latterly by *Glen Gower*, seen here in a postcard view purchased by one of the authors in a back street shop in the French port many years after the sailings had ceased and she had gone to the breakers.

In 2006 a special charter took *Balmoral* to Rotterdam for a yacht race.

Balmoral berthed in the River Maas at Rotterdam on that occasion.

Red Funnel has a long history of offering cruises to see the great liners at Southampton, as evidenced by this view of *Queen Mary's* return to Southampton after breaking the Blue Riband on 31 August 1936. From left to right, the paddle steamers are: *Gracie Fields*, the Southern Railway's *Whippingham*, *Lorna Doone* and *Balmoral*.

Balmoral has often offered trips to see Cunard's *Queen Elizabeth 2* arrive and depart. Here she is seen departing from the Clyde on her penultimate visit to the river of her birth on 20 September 2007.

On the final call of *QE2* on 5 October 2008, HMS *Manchester* also met the Cunarder, and is seen running alongside *Balmoral* off the Cowal coast between Innellan and Dunoon.

A water spray from a fire-fighting tug later the same day off the Tail of the Bank, while *Queen Elizabeth 2* was followed up firth, 5 October 2008.

Off Kilcreggan on the occasion of a special sailing for the final call of the *Queen Elizabeth 2* on 5 October 2008.

On the farewell cruise round Britain of the *QE2*, trips were planned by *Balmoral* to see her from Liverpool and Cork for her calls there, and from Bangor, Portaferry, Donaghadee and Belfast for her call at Belfast, as advertised in this handbill. Unfortunately, due to stormy weather conditions, none of these trips took place.

Chapter 11: Miscellany

Above: A line-up of present and former pursers and other personnel at the gangway. From left to right: Lionel Vaughan (shop), Derek Gawn (purser), the late John Holyoak (Balmoral Restoration Fund) Tony Gamblin (current purser), Julian Bowden Green (purser), Captain Kit Lee, Patrick Murrell (purser, shop)

Right: A chalked notice for an afternoon cruise by *Balmoral* at St George's Pier, Menai Bridge.

STEAMER BOOKING OFFICE
M.V. "BALMORAL"
Today at 2.30 P.M.
Cruise, due back at
5.45 P.M.
FARE ADULT 75p
CHILD 40p

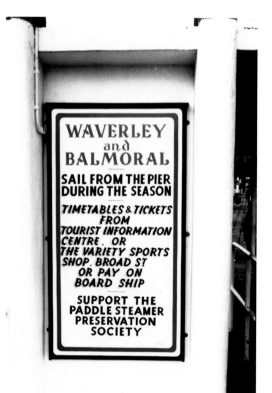

Above: Passengers enjoying the sunshine and the shelter of the aft promenade deck.

Left: An advertisement for *Waverley* and *Balmoral* on Ilfracombe Pier in 1987.

Above: Two special men in the history of the coastal pleasure steamer, Ian Muir and Ian McMillan, in the *Balmoral*'s engine room with the old Newbury Sirron engines, which by this time it was getting increasingly hard to maintain and to source spare parts for. The late Ian Muir was invaluable to *Waverley*, and former WEL chairman McMillan is still with the company today.

Right: Fixing some part or other on the top of the old Sirron engines.

One of the Sirron engines being lifted out of *Balmoral* when she was being re-engined in David Abel's shipyard in Bristol in April 2003. Note the funnel removed.

Balmoral with a starboard list, because her port engine has been removed, at David Abel's shipyard. Note that she has no funnel at this point.

Right: The new Danish-built Grenaa diesels in situ and the engine room totally upgraded.

Below: The present dining saloon, which is the third design since the area was created in 1986. The chairs were sourced from the same manufacturer in Poland which had supplied the original chairs for *Balmoral* when she was built in 1949.

Compare the previous picture to the white tablecloths of the dining saloon on *Gracie Fields* from the 1937 *Red Funnel Stuff* company guidebook.

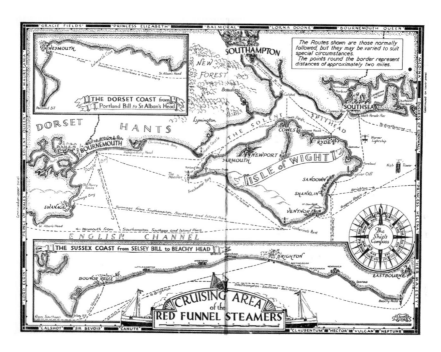

This map of the Red Funnel cruising area is replicated in a couple of mirrors in *Balmoral*'s lower bar and dining saloon.

The 1990s saw a wide variety of funnel colours on *Balmoral*. Here, off the Manx coast in 1991, she shows the traditional Campbell white funnel with black cowl.

The short-lived, buff, green-topped funnel with the gold band used in 1994.

Top: On the River Usk, showing her black funnel cowl, on 13 August 1999.

Below: *Balmoral*'s specially painted red funnel in September 2001, when she was chartered to the BBC for the filming of the series *Crowdie and Cream* at Tarbert, Loch Fyne, where she represented MacBrayne's *Clydesdale*.

That's the journey on board a most historic ship over the past sixty years. We hope it has given an insight into the varied career of *Balmoral* the way you would. If you have yet to sample a cruise, it is a 'must do'.

Only by sailing on her or by giving through WSN Co.'s Gift Aid scheme, can you contribute to her survival. To support *Balmoral* (and *Waverley*) join the Paddle Steamer Preservation Society: John Anderson, 10 Stockfield Close, Haslemere, Bucks, HP15 7LA

For details of sailing times, fares, etc contact Waverley Excursions: 36 Lancefield Quay, Glasgow, G3 8HA

The following organisations support the sailings of *Balmoral*:

Clyde River Steamer Club Eric J. Schofield, 67 Atholl Drive, Giffnock, Glasgow, G46 6QW

Coastal Cruising Association Mrs Margaret Skee, 9 Newton Terrace, Newton Street, Greenock, PA16 8ST

Many thanks *Balmoral*. 'Finished with engines'; and here's to your centenary and beyond.